the

yadayada

Prayer Journal

the yadayada

Prayer Journal

Neta & Dave Jackson

INTEGRITY®

P U B L I S H E R S

Nashville

Contents

A Letter from Neta

Dear Sister,

A prayer journal to go with a series of fiction novels? Whoever heard of such a thing! And yet, as my husband and I began to dig through the three Yada Yada Prayer Group novels for excerpts, I began to get excited! Whoa! Again and again passages leapt out at me that challenged me to think about the themes raised by these novels: grace . . . forgiveness . . . redemption. *Yes!* I said. Reading these novels was just the first course. We need to chew on some of these things to really extract the spiritual nourishment God has planted in them.

So are you ready to join me for a devotional journey, along with the fictional sisters in the Yada Yada Prayer Group?

Here's how it works. There are sixty devotionals. If you use this journal at least twenty days a month, that means we'll be reflecting and praying together for about three months, give or take a hurricane, the birth of triplets, or remodeling your kitchen—any of which might slow you down—or Jesus returning again, in which case it won't matter.

Each day begins with an excerpt from one of the Yada Yada novels, followed by a **Reflection,** from my heart to yours. The blank lines that follow are for your own reflections. A scripture **From the Word** and a **Prayer** suggestion (with blank lines for your own personal prayers) wrap up our time together.

Dear sister, thank you for joining me on this devotional journey. Make it your own, just between you and Jesus. Share it if you want to, hug it to your heart if you'd rather. If we don't meet here on earth, we'll meet in heaven and then we'll *really* "yada yada" (know and be known) and "yadah yadah" (sing and give praise to God). Yea, God!

Your Sister in Christ,
Neta Jackson

Section 1

Grace

Day 1—*Friendly, but Not Friends*

In Des Moines, Iowa, where my family lives, I grew up on missionary stories from around the world—the drumbeats of Africa . . . the rickshaws of China . . . the forests of Ecuador. Somehow it was so easy to imagine myself one day sitting on a stool in the African veld, surrounded by eager black faces, telling Bible stories with flannel-graph figures. Once, when I told Denny about my fantasy, he snorted and said we'd better learn how to relate across cultures in our own city before winging across the ocean to "save the natives."

—*The Yada Yada Prayer Group*, p. 5

Reflection

Okay, I admit it. It's easier to imagine doing great things for God in some other place or culture—while failing to realize that those same opportunities (and cultural challenges) are often only a few blocks away or just across town. I'm challenged by what Jesus said in Luke 16:10: "Whoever can be trusted with very little can also be trusted with much."

I want to be "trusted with much," but I'm no superhero; I can't get from here to there in a single bound! God wants me to be faithful in the smaller things and willing to take small steps to share God's love outside my usual circle of friends and neighbors.

How about you? How would you like to be used by God? What are the "small things" you can do right now, right where you are, to begin walking toward that vision? What is holding you back?

_____

_____

_____

_____

_____

_____

_____

_____

From the Word

Then the righteous will answer him, "Lord, when did we see you hungry and feed you, or thirsty and give you something to drink? When did we see you a stranger and invite you in, or needing clothes and clothe you? When did we see you sick or in prison and go to visit you?"

The King will reply, "I tell you the truth, whatever you did for one of the least of these brothers of mine, you did for me." (Matthew 25:37–40)

Prayer

Pray that God would show you one small step you can take to reach out to someone different from yourself. Who might that be? Include his or her name in your prayer.

_____

_____

_____

_____

_____

_____

_____

_____

Day 2—*Who Did God Create Me to Be?*

I scrunched down in my seat, hiding behind the women in front of me. Destiny? Who had time to think about destiny! Trying to keep up with a classroom of thirty third-graders, half of whom could barely speak English, much less read it, two teens with raging hormones, a happy-go-lucky husband who was more generous than thrifty, and a full schedule of church meetings at Uptown Community, I felt lucky to wake up each morning knowing what day it was.

—*The Yada Yada Prayer Group*, p. 14

Reflection

Ouch! That's me. I so easily let the cares and busyness of life over-whelm me until I can't see the forest because of all those pesky trees. Especially when my kids were young, I often felt reduced to "survival mode" with no sense of a larger purpose. (I still struggle with letting the urgent crowd out the important.)

Does this sound familiar? List a few things in your life that have this effect on you. Do you feel like you're moving forward or just spinning your wheels? To what larger purpose might God be calling you?

As you reflect on God's larger purpose for your life, remember Esther. With no choice in the matter, she ended up in the palace as a trophy wife, but God had a bigger idea. He had put her there "for such a time as this." God gave her a larger purpose: to save the lives of her people. She had destiny!

_____

_____

_____

_____

_____

_____

From the Word

I called you by name when you did not know me. I am the
LORD; there is no other God. I have prepared you, even
though you do not know me. (Isaiah 45:4–5 NLT)

Prayer

∽ Thank God that He has known you by name since
before you were born and that He has prepared you—is
preparing you—"for such a time as this." Identify three
major areas in your life, and ask God to clarify what His
destiny is for you in each area. If you are uncomfortable
with the routine you've slipped into, talk to Him about it.

_____

_____

_____

_____

_____

_____

_____

_____

Day 3—*Letting Others See the Real You*

"Who, me?" Florida shrugged. "Oh well, why not. My name is Florida Hickman. I'm five years saved and five years sober, thank the *Lord*. Got three kids. Two are living with me right now; the oldest one is ADD, otherwise they doin' good. My husband works full time"—she gave a little laugh— "lookin' for work."

. . . "But thank God, I got my GED, passed the civil service exam last year, and got a job at the Chicago post office that puts food on the table. So I can't complain. I'm blessed!" She smiled sweetly at the Hispanic lady. "Now you."

—*The Yada Yada Prayer Group*, p. 20

Reflection

- Be honest: are you more like Jodi or Florida when it comes to letting other people see "the real you"? Why are you that way? (Me, I'm a blabbermouth, jumping in with both feet—putting my "best feet" forward, of course, and sometimes getting both feet in my mouth.)

_____

_____

_____

_____

_____

- How do you respond to people who are open and transparent? How do you respond to people who are guarded? Why do they affect you that way? What effect do different approaches have on building relationships?

_____

_____

_____

_____

_____

_____

_____

_____

_____

From the Word

Fearing people is a dangerous trap, but to trust the LORD means safety. (Proverbs 29:25 NLT)

Prayer

> *"Lord, help me be more willing to let others see the real me as You made me and as I am, even if that means revealing some embarrassing details about still being a work in progress."*

✎   Talk to the Lord about those areas, and ask Him for grace to let them be known.

_____

_____

_____

_____

_____

_____

_____

_____

_____

As I soaked in the murmured prayers and gazed around the group, I suddenly noticed something.

Nails. Lots of painted fingernails, no two shades of red alike. Not only that, but every dark hand, whether African or Caribbean or American, had painted nails. I glanced on either side of me. Even Avis and Florida. But most of the pale hands—Yo-Yo for sure, but also Ruth and me and Hoshi— had bald nails, though Hoshi's looked carefully manicured with very white moon-slivers at the tips.

Stu was the exception. Her nails were long, blue, and glittery.

Good grief, Jodi! Stop it! I squeezed my eyes shut. *Dear God, I'm sorry for getting distracted. Help me to stay focused . . . focused on You.*

—*The Yada Yada Prayer Group,* pp. 44–45

Reflection

Some people may find it easy to remain focused during prayer. But if you battle distractions like Jodi does (yes, me too), at least we can be counted among Jesus' disciples—they even fell asleep in the garden on the night of His betrayal!

∾   Reflect on Jesus' gentle rebuke: "Couldn't you stay awake and watch with me even one hour? Keep alert and pray. Otherwise temptation will overpower you. For though the spirit is willing enough, the body is weak!" (Matthew 26:40–41 NLT). How would you respond to Jesus if this rebuke were directed to you?

_____
_____
_____
_____
_____
_____
_____
_____

From the Word

For we do not have a high priest who is unable to sympathize
with our weaknesses, but we have one who has been tempted
in every way, just as we are—yet was without sin. (Hebrews
4:15)

Prayer

Pray with grateful thanks that Jesus understands our ten-
dency to be distracted, and then approach God with confidence that you can find grace in your time of need.

_____
_____
_____
_____
_____
_____
_____
_____
_____

Day 5—*Praying to Win the Lottery?*

I corralled my thoughts and tried to focus on Chanda, the Jamaican woman who said she cleaned houses on the North Shore. Had been doing it for ten years, had a good clientele. But the focus on "living into your destiny" had stirred up feelings of dissatisfaction. "I wan' to be doin' someting else, but I don' know what," she said. "Got tree kids, no mon. It's hard to jump the train."

[Later Jodi hears Chanda on the phone:] "Tomas? . . . Did ya check me lottery numbers on this morning? . . . On the refrigerator door, where they always put! . . . Gwan do it . . . Yes, I wait. . . .

"Ya sure? . . . Ya double-check? . . . I was *sartin* I gwan be a winna . . . 'cause I been prayin' 'bout it all weekend."

—*The Yada Yada Prayer Group,* pp. 48, 50

Reflection

Sure, go ahead and chuckle at Chanda—for about two seconds. Then join me in a little guilt trip about all the times *we've* prayed for God to answer us as though He were in the business of fixing the lottery! Seriously, don't we sometimes treat God like a sugar daddy, hoping we can wheedle some special blessings our way?

✎ Yet God *does* want us to ask for what we need! (Check out Matthew 21:22 and Philippians 4:6–7.) Hmm. Feels a bit confusing. What do you think about that phrase "whatever you ask" in Matthew 21:22?

_____

_____

_____

_____

From the Word

When you ask, you do not receive, because you ask with wrong motives, that you may spend what you get on your pleasures. . . . But he gives us more grace. That is why Scripture says: "God opposes the proud but gives grace to the humble." Submit your-selves, then, to God. (James 4:3, 6–7)

Pray

- What are three things you are seeking God for? What are your motives in each? Write these below.

_____

_____

_____

_____

_____

_____

- Would you feel God had answered you in a generous way if He were simply to give you "more grace"? Take a moment to thank God, regardless of how He answers your prayers.

_____

_____

_____

_____

_____

_____

_____

_____

Day 6—*A Sacrifice of Praise*

"I want you to close your eyes and start thinking about *what Jesus has done for YOU.* Some of you were on drugs, your mind so muddled you had no idea what day it was, much less how many kids you had. . . .

"And *some* of you thought you were pretty good. You kept all the major commandments and managed to avoid the big mistakes. But let me tell you—you were *still* going to hell until Jesus saved you!" . . .

The worship leader was hollering now. "Maybe you don't feel like praising today. Praise anyway. Give God a *sacrifice!* Maybe you don't feel like dancing. Dance anyway! Give God a *sacrifice!*"

—*The Yada Yada Prayer Group,* pp. 53–54

Reflection

Bad girl or good girl: which label would you wear on your shirt? Are you like me, someone who has pretty much kept all the major commandments and managed to avoid big mistakes—and felt kinda smug about it too? Or are you someone who has felt so rotten about yourself that you can't believe God's grace is really sufficient to make you whole?

∾ Either way, take a few moments to jot down *what Jesus has done for YOU.* (Remember, all our "self-righteousness" is about as putrid as dirty rags. Check out Isaiah 64:6—if you dare! And the so-called bad girls? Check out the good news in John 5:24!)

_____

_____

_____

_____

_____

_____

From the Word

For all have sinned and fall short of the glory of God.
(Romans 3:23)

The wages of sin is death, but the gift of God is eternal life in
Christ Jesus our Lord. (Romans 6:23)

A Prayer for You

*"Lord Jesus, You love the sister using this prayer journal. It doesn't matter
to You if she's a 'bad girl' or a 'good girl'—because none of us is holy
enough to come into God's presence on our own. Thank You that all Your
grace and all Your mercy and all Your love is just waiting to be poured
out on this woman. She is precious in Your sight. Help her to let go of the
sins that are dragging her down, so that she can walk with her chin up,
eyes alight, a song in her heart because she is Your beloved one!"*

   ❧   And now, dear one, write your own prayer of thanks.

_____

_____

_____

_____

_____

_____

Day 7—*A Sacrifice for . . .*

I sighed again. *You're a big hypocrite, Jodi Baxter. Not twenty-four hours ago you were thinking the idea of five hundred women dressing up like Oscar night was pretty silly. You were pining for the small, casual women's retreats up at Camp Timberlee. Now you have a chance to loosen up at this big women's conference—with a dozen other women willing to be just as casual—and you're having a fit. . . .*

Sacrifice.

The word popped into my head so strongly I looked around, thinking I'd heard a voice. *Sacrifice . . . a sacrifice of praise.* I frowned. What did that have to do with anything? *A sacrifice for Yo-Yo.*

—*The Yada Yada Prayer Group,* p. 60

Reflection

It hit me right in the middle of a worship service recently, when the worship leader talked about giving God a "sacrifice of praise": *a sacrifice means that something dies so that something else can live.* Whoa! That opened up a lot of possibilities of things in me that might need to die: my ego, my pride, my laziness, what makes *me* comfortable . . .

≈   Think about it a moment. What would *you* have to sacrifice to give God uninhibited praise? Has God nudged you to do something recently that might call for a sacrifice on your part? (This is a private journal—go ahead, jot it down. No one's looking.)

_____

_____

_____

_____

_____

_____

_____

_____

_____

From the Word

Through Jesus, therefore, let us continually offer to God a sacrifice of praise—the fruit of lips that confess his name. And do not forget to do good and to share with others, for with such sacrifices God is pleased. (Hebrews 13:15–16)

Prayer

Pray for the courage to give God a "sacrifice of praise" today. (Maybe you don't *feel* like praising today!) Also ask God to give you the grace to "do good and share with others" in a sacrificial way today. What might that sacrifice entail? Pray for that specifically—and don't forget to thank Jesus for His sacrifice for you.

_____

_____

_____

_____

_____

_____

_____

Day 8—*Praying When People Are Looking*

"The rest of you—pray."

I watched her thread quickly through the doors. What did Avis mean? Pray silently to ourselves? Obviously not, because at that instant Adele launched into a loud prayer for divine protection, "whatever this emergency is about."

Nony picked up the prayer. "O God, Your Word says that we who dwell in the secret place of the Most High will abide under the shadow of the Almighty. You are our refuge and our fortress. We trust in You. Spread Your wings over Delores; let her find refuge there." . . .

I noticed several women at other tables glancing at us from time to time. No wonder. One minute we were laughing uproariously, the next praying out loud.

—*The Yada Yada Prayer Group,* p. 64

Reflection

My dad used to sing loudly in church—off-key. Didn't matter to him. He wasn't singing for the rest of us. He was singing to God! He also used to embarrass us kids by asking people if they were "saved" or by praying about something—out loud—even with other people looking. Sheesh!

Are there times you feel uncomfortable during someone else's prayer? Or maybe with the way they worship? Why? Does it seem they are drawing too much attention to themselves? Do you disagree with the content? Did you feel the prayer asked for too much? Or did you feel "unspiritual" by comparison?

_____

_____

_____

_____

_____

_____

_____

From the Word

Shout for joy to the LORD, all the earth, burst into jubilant
song with music; make music to the LORD with the harp,
with the harp and the sound of singing, with trumpets and
the blast of the ram's horn—shout for joy before the LORD,
the King. (Psalm 98:4–6)

Prayer

Pray that God will free you from anything—fear, embar-
rassment, doubt—that might hinder you in coming to
Him for any reason, at any time, in any place. Only
remember to bathe *all* your prayers in thanksgiving.

_____

_____

_____

_____

_____

_____

_____

_____

_____

Day 9—*The Illusion of Insulation*

Whenever I'd read stories in the *Chicago Tribune* about another gang shooting, it always seemed so far away, like another universe. I'd look at my Josh, whooping it up with his dad watching the Bulls or the Bears, and feel relief that I didn't have to worry about gangs. And then I'd close the paper and forget.

But this time I'd met a mother, a mother like me . . . and I couldn't forget.

—*The Yada Yada Prayer Group*, 69–70

Reflection

"Walk a mile in someone else's shoes." That image helps me remember the importance of taking time to see things from another person's perspective. To put myself in his or her shoes. To not presume my own life experience is normative. To not assume my way, or my ideas, or my opinions are best.

⌇ Intimately knowing a person whose life experience is different than your own can change your attitudes. Name a person—in your place of work, or your school, or your neighborhood or town—whose culture, economics, or race is different than your own. How well do you know what happens to this person from week to week—her loves, her fears, her challenges, her joys, her family? How might you take a step or two to "walk in her shoes"?

_____

_____

_____

_____

_____

_____

_____

_____

_____

From the Word

But God has combined the members of the body and has given greater honor to the parts that lacked it, so that there should be no division in the body, but that its parts should have equal concern for each other. If one part suffers, every part suffers with it; if one part is honored, every part rejoices with it. Now you are the body of Christ, and each one of you is a part of it. (1 Corinthians 12:24–27)

Prayer

Pray that God would guide you in making friends with another part of His body—someone culturally, economically, or racially different than yourself. What would *you* need to do for that to happen? Pray for that!

_____

_____

_____

_____

_____

_____

_____

_____

"Jodi? Are you okay? . . . I heard a moan, and just wanted to be sure you're all right."

"Yeah, I'm okay. Just, you know, worried . . ."

Avis came over to my side of the bed and sat down. I was still on my knees. "We don't have to worry," she said quietly. "God is in control. He's bigger than this. He's bigger than the enemy. He's already won this battle."

I frowned in the dark. How could she say that? What if José died—or was already dead? I mean, sure, God was "in control" —but bad things still happened.

—*The Yada Yada Prayer Group,* p. 72

Reflection

I met Sister Edna at a women's retreat recently, and something she said stuck in my mind: "I believed in God all my life—but I didn't *believe God.*" Whew! Those words keep running through my mind: Do I really *believe God?* Believe His promises? Believe what the Word says? Believe that God is in control—even when it looks like the world (or my life) is spinning out of control? What does that mean? Am I just playing mind games, sounding superspiritual? Or . . . do I really *believe God?*

☞ What about you? Do you *believe God*—or do you just believe *in* God? Is there a particular circumstance in which you are having trouble believing God's promises? Write down the areas of your life in which you struggle to believe God is in control—or even cares. (Remember, this is just between you and God. He can take it.)

_____

_____

_____

_____

_____

From the Word

And we know that in all things God works for the good of
those who love him, who have been called according to his
purpose. For those God foreknew he also predestined to be
conformed to the likeness of his Son, that he might be the
firstborn among many brothers. And those he predestined,
he also called; those he called, he also justified; those he justified, he also glorified. (Romans 8:28–30)

Prayer

Pray that your faith would grow from simply believing in
God to *believing God*. Pray for the grace to embrace God's
purpose in the circumstances He has allowed to come into
your life, for confidence in His presence walking with you
through it, and for spiritual eyes to see how He is helping
you grow into the likeness of His Son. Thank Him for His
promises to you. (Don't know how to do that? Personalize
Romans 8:28–30 above, making it your prayer.)

_____

_____

_____

_____

_____

Crisis was over.

But I heard Yo-Yo's voice again. "What are you guys going to do? . . ."

"How do you mean, do?" Ruth asked in that funny, backward way of hers.

"About Delores. What are you going to do about Delores?"

There was an awkward silence, which Yo-Yo took as an invitation. "You guys been talkin' all night to the Big Guy upstairs about Delores's boy. Looks like He gave a pretty good answer . . . for starters. But everybody just goin' to go home? Like this prayer group never happened? Delores might still need you, you know."

—*The Yada Yada Prayer Group*, p. 77

Reflection

How easy it is to drop out when the crisis is over! I know I can kick into high gear to help or pray or be there for a friend or neighbor in the moment of obvious need—but soon forget that after the hospital stay, after the funeral, after the move, even after the wedding, support is still needed.

To help me be faithful in prayer over the long haul, I recently created a "Daughter Prayer List," which includes about fifteen names of mothers who have asked prayer for their daughters—for whatever reason. About once a week, I pray through the entire list, even when I know a crisis has passed. This list is also a reminder to occasionally send an e-mail or pick up the phone to ask for an update or just to say, "I'm still praying."

⇒ Do you have a friend or relative who recently experienced a crisis or prayer need? Would a phone call now, just to ask, "How ya doin'?" be supportive? (List a few others who need ongoing prayer support.)

_____

_____

_____

_____

From the Word

But a Samaritan, as he traveled, came where the man was; and when he saw him, he took pity on him. He went to him and bandaged his wounds, pouring on oil and wine. Then he put the man on his own donkey, took him to an inn and took care of him. The next day he took out two silver coins and gave them to the innkeeper. "Look after him," he said, "and when I return, I will reimburse you for any extra expense you may have." (Luke 10:33–35)

Prayer

Pray that your concern for other people will not be a flash in the pan. Pray that the Holy Spirit will keep fresh in your heart and mind those who happen to be out of sight. When God brings a person to mind during the day, pray for him or her right then and there, no matter what you're doing.

_____

_____

_____

_____

_____

Day 12—*Uncommunicated Expectations*

Slipping off my shoes and hanging up my jacket in the hall closet, I could hear the television in the living room—a baseball game, no doubt. Then I heard male laughter—several adult voices.

Rats. Denny had company.

I could almost taste the resentment that surged upward from my gut. Didn't Denny know I'd be home about now? That we hadn't seen each other for two whole days and nights? That I'd want some time together to catch up with each other?

—*The Yada Yada Prayer Group*, p. 88

Reflection

Uncommunicated expectations? Hey, I had *that* down to a science, especially when I first got married. ("If he really loved me, he would *know* . . .") I was pretty good at vague requests too. ("Sure wish people wouldn't leave their junk lying around.")

In the above scene from *The Yada Yada Prayer Group*, Jodi is upset that Denny wasn't waiting—alone—for her return, something she had never asked of him but just hoped he would know she wanted.

✎ Sound familiar? (Aw, c'mon. I can't be the only one!) Think about the last few upsets you've had. How many can be traced back to "uncommunicated expectations"?

_____

_____

_____

_____

_____

_____

_____

_____

_____

_____

_____

_____

From the Word

Ask and it will be given to you; seek and you will find; knock
and the door will be opened to you. For everyone who asks
receives; he who seeks finds; and to him who knocks, the
door will be opened. (Matthew 7:7–8)

Prayer

Pray that you would be willing and able to verbalize your
needs and requests first to the Lord, but also to others
around you—at the same time being willing to accept
their responses.

_____

_____

_____

_____

_____

_____

_____

_____

_____

_____

Day 13—*Well, Why Not?*

This morning I pulled [my New Testament] out. In my head, I could hear Nony "praying Scripture," one verse after the other. I felt an inner longing to be that full of God's Word, so that it came pouring out like that.

Well, why not?

I opened the book and turned to the Psalms, included at the back. The pages fell open to Psalm 95. My eyes skimmed a few verses silently . . . *Come, let us sing for joy to the Lord; let us shout aloud to the Rock of salvation.*

I was struck by the irony. Reading "sing for joy" and "shout aloud" silently—that was me, all right. But if Florida or Nony were standing in my shoes right now, they'd take "Sing!" and "Shout!" pretty literally.

Well, why not?

—*The Yada Yada Prayer Group*, p. 104

Reflection

I grew up among Christians who felt pretty smug about taking Scripture "literally." Yet we didn't take scriptures about praising God very literally. Shouting? Dancing? Lifting up our hands? Are you kidding? We got more excited at pep rallies and watching games on TV than we did in church. I've had to wonder, *What am I trying to protect with my dignified restraint in worship?*

    What forms of worship are you most comfortable with? What makes you uncomfortable? Does your worship line up with scriptures about praise and worship? What area of worship would you like to grow in? What is hindering you?

_____

_____

_____

_____

_____

_____

_____

From the Word

David said to Michal, "It was before the LORD, who chose
me [that I danced] . . . I will celebrate before the LORD. I will
become even more undignified than this, and I will be humil-
iated in my own eyes." (2 Samuel 6:21–22)

A Prayer to Share

*"Lord Jesus, You have done so much for me! Heaven instead of hell!
Mercy instead of judgment! Taking my punishment for my sins! How
can I sit still or keep from shouting? Release me from my inhibitions so
that I can praise You fully, with my whole being, even if it means
becoming 'undignified'! Thank You, Jesus. Thank You!"*

Add to this prayer as you wish.

_____

_____

_____

_____

_____

_____

_____

_____

Day 14—*Back-Talking "The Enemy"*

"We're claiming *victory* for José's life, Father God! Right now, in the name of Jesus! Satan, you can't have him!—or his brother, or his sisters, or anyone in his family. Hands off, Satan! This is God's child!"

I couldn't help sneaking a peek through my eyelashes at the visitors for Bed One as Avis back-talked "the enemy." The two older ladies stared open-mouthed in our direction. I didn't look at Mr. Enriques to see how he was reacting to Avis's prayer. But I closed my eyes again, realizing it didn't really matter. Avis wasn't trying to offend anyone—but she believed in the importance of prayer so much that she just did it, even if it did.

Oh God, how many people have I not *prayed for or with because I was too afraid of offending somebody?*

—*The Yada Yada Prayer Group,* p. 119

Reflection

I was moaning a while ago to a sister-friend about a sore back, and she asked, "Have you asked your husband to pray for you? Lay hands on you? Anoint you with oil?" Duh. I have to admit, prayer is not always my first response to a problem. Complaining, worry, painkiller, talking about it . . . oh yeah! Prayer!

But that's changing. I'm learning—still learning—that prayer is the most important thing I can do in any circumstance, whether for myself or for someone else. Now when someone calls and asks me to pray about something, I say, "Let's pray right now, right on the phone."

 ❧ Ask yourself, Do I believe in the power of prayer? How important is prayer in the way I face the daily challenges of my life? In the challenges facing our nation? The

world? On a scale of one to ten, how would my family
rank my willingness to pray whenever about whatever?

_____

_____

_____

_____

_____

From the Word

The seventy-two returned with joy and said, "Lord, even the
demons submit to us in your name."

[Jesus] replied, "I saw Satan fall like lightning from
heaven. I have given you authority to trample on snakes and
scorpions and to overcome all the power of the enemy; nothing will harm you. However, do not rejoice that the spirits
submit to you, but rejoice that your names are written in
heaven." (Luke 10:17–20)

Prayer

Ask God for the faith to really believe that Jesus has given
us authority to rebuke Satan in circumstances both large
and small.

_____

_____

_____

_____

_____

Day 15—*To Know and Be Known*

[An e-mail to the Yada Yada Prayer Group from Ruth]

So who's the brilliant person who came up with the name, Yada Yada? I knew it meant something. I looked it up in my Hebrew dictionary. "Yada: to perceive, understand, acquire knowledge, know, discern." And a whole lot more. Here's one I like: "To be known, make oneself known, to be familiar." And another: "To distinguish (yada) between right and wrong."

If we add an "h" it gets even better. "Yadah: to speak out, to confess; to praise; to sing; to give thanks." Later it says Yadah "essentially means to acknowledge . . . the nature and work of God."

—*The Yada Yada Prayer Group*, p. 125

Reflection

Numerous people think I must be a *Seinfeld* fan because I used the phrase "yada yada" as the title of my novels. Confession: I've never seen an episode of *Seinfeld*. I didn't know the show made that phrase famous. Rather, I was intrigued by a worship dance group in our church called Yadah, Yadah, Yadah. When I asked what it meant, the director pointed me to how "Yadah" and "Yada" are used in Scripture (see quote above). *Whoa!* I thought. *What a great name for a prayer group.* "To know and be known." "To give praise to God."

꙳ Given these meanings, consider: Who "yadas" you? Who do you "yada"? And who do you "yadah"?

_____

_____

_____

_____

_____

_____

From the Word

This is the message we have heard from him and declare to you: God is light; in him there is no darkness at all. If we claim to have fellowship with him yet walk in the darkness, we lie and do not live by the truth. But if we walk in the light, as he is in the light, we have fellowship with one another, and the blood of Jesus, his Son, purifies us from all sin.

If we claim to be without sin, we deceive ourselves and the truth is not in us. If we confess our sins, he is faithful and just and will forgive us our sins and purify us from all unrighteousness. If we claim we have not sinned, we make him out to be a liar and his word has no place in our lives. (1 John 1:5–10)

Prayer

Ask God to give you the courage to let yourself be truly known by some trusted believers, to "walk in the light," to come out of the darkness of fear and self-doubt so you can know true fellowship.

_____

_____

_____

_____

_____

Day 16—*A Day Late and a Dollar Short*

The service was over, and I was introducing Stu to the people around us when I saw several folks head for the kitchen. I stopped in midsentence: the potluck! And my casserole was still sitting on top of the stove, stone cold.

"Jodi? Are you okay?" Stu looked at me quizzically.

"No . . . yes! Yes, I'm fine. Denny?" I plucked on my husband's sleeve. "Could you introduce Stu to some folks? I've . . . I'll be back in a minute."

I didn't head for the kitchen. I headed for the women's bathroom. . . .

I locked the door and sank down on the toilet seat. I wasn't sure whether to laugh or cry. Why did I forget today of all days? With Miss Do-Everything-Right visiting. Why did I always end up feeling a day late and a dollar short when Stu was around?

—*The Yada Yada Prayer Group*, pp. 187–188

Reflection

Yes, I know *who we are* is more important than *what we do*. But aren't we all tempted to base our identity to some extent on *what we do well*? (Don't tell me I'm the only one again!) Are you musical? A good organizer? Good at sports? A dynamo speaker? A straight-A student?

But here's the rub: there will always be someone who does what we do best—even better than we do. (How fair is that?) It's no skin off our nose to applaud someone who's good in a totally different area. But it's not easy ending up, like Jodi, feeling "a day late and a dollar short" next to Miss Got-It-All-Together.

∾ In what kind of situations do you end up feeling most
inadequate? Around whom? How have you handled these
inadequate feelings in the past?

_____

_____

_____

_____

_____

_____

_____

From the Word

For by the grace given me I say to every one of you: Do not
think of yourself more highly than you ought, but rather
think of yourself with sober judgment, in accordance with the
measure of faith God has given you. (Romans 12:3)

Prayer

∾ Ask God to help you find your identity in who you are in
Christ—spotless, His bride, His beloved one, worth dying
for, redeemed. Pray that your gifts and talents will be used
to serve others and bring glory to God (not yourself).

_____

_____

_____

_____

_____

_____

_____

Day 17—*Surprised By* . . .

I picked up a copy of *O*—Oprah's magazine—from among the available reading materials [in Adele's Hair and Nails]: *Ebony, Jet,* and *Essence,* plus several issues of neighborhood newspapers. And a Bible.

"Whose CD is that she's got on? Kirk Franklin's new one?"

"Sounds like Fred Hammond to me."

I'm not sure which surprised me more: the Bible on the coffee table, the gospel music flooding the salon, or the coffeepot, half-full, plugged in on a little table beside the love seat. A cake server snuggled among the Styrofoam cups, powdered creamer, and packets of sugar revealed some kind of cake or pastry under its glass lid. Everything looked so . . . inviting. Sit down. Stay awhile.

—*The Yada Yada Prayer Group,* p. 200

Reflection

A friend of mine was told recently by her boss to take the phrase "Have a blessed day!" off her office answering machine. (It might be "offensive" to some of her clients.) Sheesh! Such mild speech is considered more odious than foul language in some segments of our society, as are other public expressions of faith. Many of us are so cowed by the majority culture that we don't realize that some minority cultures enjoy much greater freedom to express their faith. (Witness the public Gospel Fests in many cities.)

How might you make more connections with believers from other cultures? What can we learn from other worship styles and expressions of our Christian faith?

_____

_____

_____

_____

_____

_____

_____

From the Word

And they sang a new song with these words: "You are worthy
to take the scroll and break its seals and open it. For you were
killed, and your blood has ransomed people for God from
every tribe and language and people and nation. And you
have caused them to become God's Kingdom and his priests.
And they will reign on the earth." (Revelation 5:9–10 NLT)

Prayer

Pray for discernment in how to be bold in your faith while
being sensitive to others. Ask God for the willingness to
step outside your own spiritual comfort zone and become
more comfortable with other believers "from every tribe
and language and people and nation," with the grace to
receive as well as to _give_ the gifts we have to offer each
other.

_____

_____

_____

_____

_____

_____

_____

I hauled in the rest of the groceries like a queen bee with her stinger in backward. Now Denny was not only "having a beer with the guys" while watching a game, but stocking up the refrigerator! (*Stomp, stomp, stomp* across the back porch.) What was he stocking up *for?* Florida's party? Over my dead body. (*Slam* the car door.) How did he buy them anyway? *I* had the car. (*Slam* the back door.) And what's with the missing bottle? Drinking by himself? In the middle of the day? (*Slam* the refrigerator door)—

"Jodi? What in the world . . . ?"

I whirled around. Denny was standing in the kitchen doorway in his jeans, barefoot and shirtless, leaning on one arm against the doorpost. He looked pretty yummy—but I was *not* going to be distracted from my anger.

—*The Yada Yada Prayer Group*, p. 209

Reflection

Why is it so much easier to see the other person's fault rather than my own? As I get older (and hopefully wiser), I have had to admit that *almost always* a breakdown in a relationship has more than one side to the story, and that I'm a contributor.

∾   Is there someone in your family or church or office whose faults drive you to distraction? How do you respond to this person? (Could that be part of the problem?)

_____

_____

_____

_____

_____

_____

_____

_____

_____

_____

From the Word

Why do you look at the speck of sawdust in your brother's
eye and pay no attention to the plank in your own eye? How
can you say to your brother, "Let me take the speck out of
your eye," when all the time there is a plank in your own eye?
You hypocrite, first take the plank out of your own eye, and
then you will see clearly to remove the speck from your
brother's eye. (Matthew 7:3–5)

Prayer

≈ Pray that you would more clearly see the world—and your
brothers and sisters—through God's eyes, letting your
heart be broken over the things that break His heart, as
well as forgiving those things He has forgiven.

_____

_____

_____

_____

_____

_____

_____

_____

_____

Day 19—*"Please! Pull the Blinds."*

The wail started in my aching gut and burst from my mouth. "Oh God, no-oo-ooo!"

"Jodi? I'm right here, girl." A cool hand touched my face, brushed the tears from my cheeks. I opened my eyes. Bright sunshine streaming in the tall window created a halo of light around Florida's dark face and tiny ringlets.

I groaned and turned my face away. *Oh God, does everybody know?* "Please! Pull the blinds."

"But the sun is shining! And look at all these flowers that keep coming in." She peered at the little cards. "Denny's folks . . . couple of families from Uptown Community—"

"I want it dark!" I snapped. I wanted to yell, *I don't want flowers, either! Don't people know I killed somebody? They oughta send the flowers to his funeral!*

"You gotta get a grip, girl, else they gonna leave you tied up so's you don't pull out all these tubes."

I refused to look at her. "Just . . . go away."

—*The Yada Yada Prayer Group*, p. 329

Reflection

I once got a devastating phone call. I was numb. I couldn't cry. I didn't know what to do. But I did go around the house and turn out all the lights. The light seemed . . . obscene somehow. Not in keeping with the darkness in my soul. I wanted so desperately to turn back the clock. To make what happened go away, to not be true.

➥   Have you ever felt this way? So burdened by a foolish mistake with dreadful consequences or a painful family situation that you could hardly bear it? Have you experienced any healing in this situation? Or is it still too painful to think about?

_____

_____

_____

_____

From the Word

"And God will wipe away every tear from their eyes; there
shall be no more death, nor sorrow, nor crying. There shall be
no more pain, for the former things have passed away." Then
He who sat on the throne said, "Behold, I make all things
new." And He said to me, "Write, for these words are true
and faithful." (Revelation 21:4–5 NKJV)

A Prayer for You

*"Lord Jesus, surround my sister in her remembered pain. Give her a
renewed sense of Your forgiveness—either to forgive or be forgiven. And
give her the grace to live in the present with both sorrow and joy—
sorrow for the sin and pain that may yet linger, and joy because that's
not the end of the story. You are faithful! You are still working out Your
purpose! Your love is full of grace and mercy! Thank You, Jesus!"*

∾   And now you continue . . .

_____

_____

_____

_____

_____

_____

Day 20—*Have Mercy on Me, a Sinner!*

Florida had said I didn't really know what it meant to be "just a sinner, saved by grace." Did she mean . . . I was like that self-inflated Pharisee? The realization was shocking. Everybody knew the Pharisees were self-righteous bad guys.

But it was true. I was proud. *Hey, God, it's me, Jodi the "good girl"! God, aren't You proud of me? . . .*

But Jesus had said that it was the *other* man, the one who *knew* he was "just a sinner," who went home forgiven.

That "other" Jodi, the one who's basically selfish and petty . . . who flies off the handle at her husband . . . who was "driving angry" a couple of weeks back . . . the one who was driving too fast for weather conditions . . . who hit a young kid . . . and killed him . . . killed him . . .

"O *God!* Have *mercy* on me! I'm just a sinner! Have *mercy!*"
—*The Yada Yada Prayer Group,* pp. 369–70

Reflection

It was so hard for me to own up to being a sinner. I mean, of course I knew (in my head) that I was a "sinner saved by grace." But I rarely felt any need for God's mercy. Hadn't I been a "good girl" all my life? Except . . . I lived with a great deal of frustration at others' faults and failings, even frequently felt down on myself for not being able to live up to my own high expectations.

I'll never forget the day God opened my eyes, and I saw that He wanted me to own up to my sins, confess them, repent, tell others I'm sorry—not because He wanted to grind my face in the mud, but so that *He* could carry them and *I* could be *free!*

❧ Think about it. Do you feel fully forgiven and free of your sins? Does your heart spill over with gratefulness for what

Jesus has done for you? Can you dance with your face lifted
upward, with no shame? If not, why not?

_____

_____

_____

_____

_____

_____

_____

From the Word

But you, O LORD, are a compassionate and gracious God,
slow to anger, abounding in love and faithfulness. Turn to me
and have mercy on me. (Psalm 86:15–16)

Prayer

Ask God for a true understanding of your sin so you can
rejoice in His grace.

_____

_____

_____

_____

_____

_____

_____

_____

_____

_____

Section 2

Forgiveness

Day 21—*Forgiving Yourself*

And thank You, Jesus, that I didn't end up in prison! Did they have hot showers in prison? Green apple shampoo? It had never occurred to me to wonder about that before I got charged with vehicular manslaughter. The prosecution tried for gross negligence, but the charges got dropped when no witnesses showed up at the hearing.

Grace. That's what it was. Only God's grace. It was an accident, yes. The boy had run out in front of my car in a pouring rain. Yet God knew I'd been driving angry. I was grateful—oh, so grateful!—that God had offered me mercy, forgiveness, and a legal acquittal, but . . . it was hard to forgive myself. After all, Jamal Wilkins was still dead; a mother was still grieving . . .

—*The Yada Yada Prayer Group Gets Down*, p. 4

Reflection

"We're not going to give you a ticket," the policewoman said to me. Though I wasn't *legally* responsible for the car accident that totaled my parents' car, stranded my mother and me in the middle of Montana, and put my father in the morgue with heart failure, my insides were still screaming, *I killed my dad! I killed my dad!* If only I had stopped the car, not tried to help my dad while traveling sixty miles per hour down the highway. *If only . . . If only . . .* Maybe God could forgive me, but I wasn't sure I could ever forgive myself.

~ Dear sister, do you blame yourself for a mistake, a failure, a sin? Is the wound still festering in your spirit? Get it out, write it down here, let God's light shine upon it. (And I will tell you a secret: Satan wants to keep us—you and me—bound up with blame and self-loathing, but Jesus wants to set us *free!*)

_____

_____

_____

_____

From the Word

When I kept silent, my bones wasted away through my groaning all day long. For day and night your hand was heavy upon me; my strength was sapped as in the heat of summer.

Then I acknowledged my sin to you and did not cover up my iniquity. I said, "I will confess my transgressions to the LORD"—and you forgave the guilt of my sin. (Psalm 32:3–5)

Prayer

Confess your failure once more to God, then *thank* Him for His great love and grace, which covers a "multitude of sins" (1 Peter 4:8). Thank Jesus that He not only took our sins upon Himself and suffered our punishment in our place, but also took away the blame and condemnation. (Oh, sister! Get up and dance! You are forgiven!)

_____

_____

_____

_____

_____

_____

_____

_____

"You rascal. When did you plan this?"

I let out my breath. "Several weeks ago—soon after the trial. I wanted to do something special to thank you for . . . for standing by me through, you know, everything."

His eyes registered pain. "Oh, Jodi, don't. Don't thank *me* for anything." He leaned forward and took both my hands, looking in my eyes so intensely I could almost feel their heat. "I've been to hell and back because of that stupid fight we had that day. But God has seen us through, *is* seeing us through, and you've forgiven me and . . ."

"Oh, Denny. You're not still blaming yourself, are you? It was *me* . . ."

We both just looked at each other, overwhelmed at the memories and feelings that were still healing. A stupid fight . . . me, late for a Yada Yada meeting, driving angry . . . a drenching thunderstorm . . . and now, a boy was dead.

—*The Yada Yada Prayer Group Gets Down*, p. 30

Reflection

Somehow I grew up thinking that good Christians don't get angry. (So what did I do with all those nasty frustrations and angry thoughts that plagued my life? I blamed it on the other guy, of course!) It took many years walking with God to finally realize that my angry response often made the situation worse, and I needed to own and take responsibility for my part in the breakdown of the relationship.

⋙ What about you? How do you usually deal with frustrations, irritations, and "stupid fights"? Stuff it, and then blow later? Let it all hang out? Excuse it as "just being honest"?

From the Word

Do not grieve the Holy Spirit of God, with whom you were
sealed for the day of redemption. Get rid of all bitterness,
rage and anger, brawling and slander, along with every form
of malice. Be kind and compassionate to one another, forgiving each other, just as in Christ God forgave you. (Ephesians
4:30–32)

Prayer

✐ Pray for the wisdom to see your anger as destructive to
yourself and others, for the courage to deal with it quickly,
and for the grace to forgive the brother or sister who
"made you mad." And praise God that because of the
blood of Jesus, you are "justified" in God's eyes—*"just as if
I'd"* never sinned.

Day 23—*The Good Ol' Days*

Whatever happened to lazy summer days watching ants on the sidewalk, sucking "Popsicles" your mom made in little plastic freezer molds, or playing question-answer games with your best friend while swinging on the deserted school playground swings?

Probably a myth by now, created in simpler times when kids had daddies, and moms stayed home. Summer day camps were no doubt better than all those kids sitting in front of the television all summer.

. . . Now that [our kids] were both teenagers, it drove me a little nuts that Josh and Amanda could easily sleep till noon if we let them. I wasn't a big fan of hanging out at the mall either. Denny solved that little problem by stopping their allowance in the summer. Any spending money they wanted they had to earn.

—*The Yada Yada Prayer Group Gets Down*, pp. 33–34

Reflection

I had a delightful childhood growing up in the 1950s. My family didn't have much money, but we were rich in family life—reading books, playing games, going camping together. We kids looked forward to college, marriage, careers—the sky was the limit! Only as a young adult did I realize the "good ol' days" of the '50s weren't so hot for my brothers and sisters of color, for whom Jim Crow discrimination, inferior schools, segregation, voting inequities, and poverty were all too prevalent. As Charles Dickens penned about another age, "It was the best of times; it was the worst of times."

    Reflect on your "good ol' days." What were the good things? The not-so-good? How about today? What are the good things? The not-so-good? Evaluate these lists in light of the scripture below.

_____

_____

_____

_____

From the Word

Therefore, I urge you, brothers, in view of God's mercy, to offer your bodies as living sacrifices, holy and pleasing to God —this is your spiritual act of worship. Do not conform any longer to the pattern of this world, but be transformed by the renewing of your mind. Then you will be able to test and approve what God's will is—his good, pleasing and perfect will. (Romans 12:1–2)

Prayer

Thank God for all His blessings that don't depend on the values of this world. Ask God to open your eyes to the "pattern[s] of this world" that threaten to consume our minds, our hearts, our families, and our wallets. Pray for a "renewed mind" in order to test and approve what God's will is.

_____

_____

_____

_____

_____

_____

"Denny? Talk to me."

He glanced sideways, a rueful smile breaking his stony expression. "Sorry, babe." He jutted his chin toward the horizon. "Don't get to see a sunset like that too often. S'pose we could catch a sunrise over Lake Michigan, if we got up early enough, but—"

"Denny." I nailed him with a look. "I mean, talk to me about what you're thinking. This is supposed to be an anniversary getaway, but I feel like I'm riding with a robot, and you're"—I waved my hand in little circles—"off in la-la land."

He sighed. "Sorry, Jodi. Don't mean to be a wet blanket. It's just . . . I don't know. I feel like I should be home combing the want ads, searching the Net, sending out résumés, whatever. I'm kicking myself that I've waited so long to look for another job, but I kept hoping that no news was good news."

—*The Yada Yada Prayer Group Gets Down*, p. 44

Reflection

We don't fool anybody, do we?—stuffing our concerns and worries, I mean. In an effort to *not* be a "wet blanket" the other night, I said nothing to the group of sisters that meets at my house for Bible study about a disturbing phone call I'd had earlier that day. But suddenly one of my sisters said, "Neta, *what*?" She could tell I wasn't myself, was holding something in. So I briefly shared and my sisters prayed for me, helping to share my burden. They were able to remind me of God's promises and to encourage me.

    Are you carrying some private worries or concerns? Why don't you tell God about them here—then let your spouse or sister-friend or prayer partner help you carry the burden.

_____

_____

_____

_____

From the Word

Do not worry about your life, what you will eat or drink; or
about your body, what you will wear. Is not life more important than food, and the body more important than clothes?
Look at the birds of the air; they do not sow or reap or store
away in barns, and yet your heavenly Father feeds them. Are
you not much more valuable than they? . . .

So do not worry, saying, "What shall we eat?" or "What
shall we drink?" or "What shall we wear?" For the pagans run
after all these things, and your heavenly Father knows that
you need them. But seek first his kingdom and his righteousness, and all these things will be given to you as well.
Therefore do not worry about tomorrow, for tomorrow will
worry about itself. Each day has enough trouble of its own.
(Matthew 6:25–26, 31–34)

Prayer

Ask God to exchange your worries with His promises.
(Here are a couple to try on for size: Hebrews 13:5–6 and
Romans 8:38–39.)

_____

_____

_____

_____

Day 25—*First Line of Defense*

I battled my own feelings: sad for MaDear, who lived through such horror at a young age, worried about why this was so heavy for Denny, and irritated that it intruded so heavily on our weekend. *You gotta help me, Lord. What are we supposed to do with this? Can't You just make it go away for a couple of days?*

Pray. That was it. Why did it still take me so long to get to the first line of defense when upsetting things happened? Avis . . . or Nony . . . maybe even Florida . . . if they were here right now they'd be circling our chairs like warriors doing battle with fear, confusion, disappointment, anger. All those sneaky spiritual fiends out to trip us up. Hadn't I learned anything in the last several months, riding life with the Yada Yada Prayer Group? I could just hear Avis say, *"It's not your battle. It's the Lord's!"*

"Denny?" I reached out for his hand. "Let's pray about all this, okay?"

—*The Yada Yada Prayer Group Gets Down*, p. 51

Reflection

"I'm not going," she said on the phone.

"What?! But you promised! I'm counting on you."

"I know, but something came up."

Oh boy, I was ticked. Disappointed. Upset. I felt like slamming the phone down and maybe a few doors for good measure. But I'm trying to live the same lessons I'm writing into my novels. (Huh. Can't let Jodi Baxter outgrow me.) So I called my husband and asked, "Could you pray with me?" First line of defense against the enemy, who wants to discourage me. And praise God! I was able to let go of my disappointment and feel God's peace. Even tell my friend, "It's okay. Things will work out."

~ What is *your* first line of defense when upsetting things happen? (Try to be honest! This is a private journal, remember.) Think back to the most recent upset and replay it in your mind. What might you have done differently?

_____

_____

_____

_____

From the Word

I exhort therefore, that, *first of all*, supplications, prayers, intercessions, and giving of thanks, be made for all men; For kings, and for all that are in authority; that we may lead a quiet and peaceable life in all godliness and honesty. For this is good and acceptable in the sight of God our Saviour. (1 Timothy 2:1–3 KJV; emphasis added)

Prayer

~ Pray that Satan would not get a foothold in your life, robbing your peace and joy by making mountains out of those pesky molehills that trip us up. Ask God for a reminder to bring things to Him *first*. And go ahead, pray about the upset that happened *just today*.

_____

_____

_____

_____

_____

_____

Day 26—*Under the Wire or Right on Time?*

Denny's news got a round of whooping and hollering when I came back into the family room grinning from ear to ear. "Thank ya, Jesus!" Florida cried. "Ain't that just like God— right on time." She punched the air in a victory salute.

More like right under the wire, I muttered to myself, remembering how much Denny had been sweating it out all summer. Yet I wasn't about to complain.

—*The Yada Yada Prayer Group Gets Down,* p. 67

Reflection

Every now and then, I'd like to sit down and hammer out a little understanding with God. *(Okay, God, I'd like answers to my prayers* right now, *thank You very much. And if it's all right with You, I'd like this prayer answered this way.)* But I'm glad God doesn't "jump to" when I'm feeling bossy in my prayers, because time and time again I've seen God has a better idea, a kingdom perspective, His way, His time. (Doesn't mean I'm always patient with His timing, but it helps to remember that "God is God all by Himself." My job is to pray and trust Him.)

✎ Have you been praying about something for a long time, feeling discouraged, doubting that God knows what He's doing? What is that prayer? (And while you're waiting, find the gospel song by Dottie Peoples, "He's an On-Time God," turn up the volume, and let this promise shake the roof *and* your doubt!)

_____

_____

_____

_____

_____

_____

_____

_____

_____

_____

_____

From the Word

The angel said, "I am Gabriel, the sentinel of God, sent especially to bring you this glad news. But because you won't believe me, you'll be unable to say a word until the day of your son's birth. Every word I've spoken to you will come true on time—God's time." (Luke 1:19–20 MSG)

Prayer

Pray for a greater measure of faith to believe God to fulfill His promises, to trust Him with your life and all that concerns you and the ones you love. Pray for patience to "wait on God" for His perfect time.

_____

_____

_____

_____

_____

_____

_____

_____

Day 27—*Thanking God First*

It occurred to me that Yada Yada had been teaching me something else I could use to start off the school year: praise and prayer. Mostly because people like Avis and Florida and Nony—well, all the sisters of color—thanked God first then looked at the facts. Ruth Garfield, lugging her Hebrew/English dictionary, had also discovered that *yadah*-spelled-with-an-h meant "to praise, to sing, to give thanks . . . to acknowledge the nature and work of God." Whew. We'd had no idea when we pulled "yada yada" out of the air, almost as a joke, as the name for our prayer group.

I peeked into the hallway to see if I could do this uninterrupted for a few minutes, then I took the printout of my incoming students and stopped by the first short desk. "Lord God, bless Ramón. Help me to love this boy like You love him." I moved to the next desk. "Thank You for LeTisha." *Hoo boy*. I was going out on a limb thanking God in advance for this one. I'd had a LeTisha in my last class, and that little girl knew more cuss words at age eight than I even knew existed.

—*The Yada Yada Prayer Group Gets Down*, p. 91

Reflection

✎ Okay, what's on your plate today . . . this week . . . coming up? A new semester? A new job? A new project? A new baby? Or maybe it's the same-old, same-old. Either way, how about taking a cue from Jodi and the Yada Yadas and "yadah"—give thanks and praise to God for each one of the people God brings into your life, even on ordinary days.

_____

_____

_____

From the Word

Here are some examples of the 114 occurrences of the word *yadah* in the Old Testament:

> This time I will praise the LORD. (Genesis 29:35)

> I will give thanks to the LORD because of his righteousness. (Psalm 7:17)

> O LORD my God, I will give you thanks forever. (Psalm 30:12)

> Let them give thanks to the LORD for his unfailing love and his wonderful deeds. (Psalm 107:8)

> Surely the righteous will praise your name. (Psalm 140:13)

> In that day you will say: "I will praise you, O LORD." (Isaiah 12:1)

Prayer

~ Give thanks and praise to God for the people who people your life today: the bus driver, the mail carrier, the crossing guard. "Yadah" God for His presence with you as you go throughout your day, for His faithfulness, and for His unfailing love.

_____

_____

_____

_____

_____

Day 28—*Divine Intervention*

It happened so fast, it was over in a blink. As the crazy woman lunged at Denny with the knife, he grabbed her wrist. The next moment she was on her back on the floor with Denny spread-eagle on top of her.

"Jodi!" he yelled. "Take the knife!"

My body parts suddenly came alive, and I scrambled toward the pair on the floor.

—*The Yada Yada Prayer Group Gets Down*, p. 107

Reflection

This is a fictionalized version of a true event involving my husband, Dave. He describes it this way in his nonfiction book, *Dial 911* (Herald Press, 1981):

> . . . in her clenched fist just before my face she held a ten-inch knife.
>
> As I recall what happened, it is like studying the individual frames of a movie film. The action was stopped, the time was extended, and I thought about far more than should fit into a person's mind in one moment. . . .
>
> I believe the Lord spoke to me then, "Grab her wrist. You will not be hurt, and you will not have to hurt her."

In fact, no one (other than an old woman whose hand the robber had previously cut) was injured in the event, and Dave was able to pin the robber to the floor until the police arrived. But then four very large cops struggled to control and take her away, and in the police car on the way to the station, she broke the handcuffs.

≈ How do you understand the Bible when it speaks of God being our defender and protector? Do you truly believe that nothing can harm you unless God allows it? How does that affect the way you live?

_____

_____

_____

_____

_____

From the Word

If you make the Most High your dwelling—even the LORD, who is my refuge—then no harm will befall you, no disaster will come near your tent. For he will command his angels concerning you to guard you in all your ways; they will lift you up in their hands, so that you will not strike your foot against a stone. (Psalm 91:9–12)

Prayer

≈ Thank God for His daily protection—accidents that didn't happen, dangers you were unaware of, uneventful flights while traveling. Pray for the safety and protection of your loved ones and friends today, whatever they're doing and wherever they are, trusting each one into God's care.

_____

_____

_____

_____

I actually found myself looking forward to the first day of school. *Hoo boy!* Now if that wasn't a miracle!

Must have been the prayer with Denny last night. We'd just held each other in the dark in the living room, pouring out all the confusion and upset we'd both been feeling, telling Jesus it had been a rotten summer. We didn't know what to do about MaDear. Getting robbed in our own home had been terrifying. We also thanked God for a lot of stuff. Like Josh and Amanda and the rest of Uptown's youth getting home safely from Mexico and having a great time building houses with Habitat for Humanity. For the strength our Yada Yada sisters had poured into both of us with their prayers and their presence during those awful days following the accident. That the charges against me got dropped, and I was healing fast. That Denny still had a job at the high school.

Once we started, it seemed like there were so many things to pray about. . . . "Good thing God is God all by Himself!" I'd muttered after our final amen.

—*The Yada Yada Prayer Group Gets Down*, pp. 137–138

Reflection

I've been known to scold total strangers for dropping litter, tell other people's children to stop running at the pool, and make the bed in the motel before checking out. "Mom!" my daughter would wail, rolling her eyes. "You're not Mother of the Universe!"

Don't you hate it when your kids are right? And I have to admit, many times I do feel overly responsible for keeping everybody happy, keeping everything on track and running smoothly. But the job is too big; I can't do it! And it helps to be reminded by my Bible study sisters that "God is God all by Himself." Our job is to pray; it's His job to run the world.

～ Feeling overly responsible right now? Can you identify
those things you are trying to control?

_____

_____

_____

_____

_____

From the Word

I am God, your God. I do not rebuke you for your sacrifices
or your burnt offerings, which are ever before me. [But] I
have no need of a bull from your stall or of goats from your
pens, for every animal of the forest is mine, and the cattle on
a thousand hills. . . . Sacrifice thank offerings to God, fulfill
your vows to the Most High, and call upon me in the day of
trouble; I will deliver you, and you will honor me. (Psalm
50:7–10, 14–15)

Prayer

～ Thank God that His purposes are for our good, not for
disaster (Jeremiah 29:11). Ask Him to help you be faithful
to the tasks, responsibilities, and relationships—small or
great—that He has given you, and trust Him with the rest.

_____

_____

_____

_____

_____

_____

Day 30—*Just Desserts?*

"So. Did Sergeant Curry say what her sentence was?"

"Yeah. Ten years for assault."

I took a sip of coffee to steady my nerves. "What does that mean? That she'll be out on parole in a measly five years?"

Denny shook his head. "Dunno. They've got 'truth in sentencing' now. Not sure when her parole could come up."

The waiter refilled our glasses of ice water, and we munched on the chips and salsa for a while in silence. So Bandana Woman got a short ride to prison. Wasn't that good news? Why did I feel so disturbed?

—*The Yada Yada Prayer Group Gets Down*, p. 186

Reflection

"But it's not *fair!*" My kids were masters of the "fairness whine" (though, to be *fair*, no more so than I was—and every other kid I've ever met). There is something deep in the human psyche that wants not only fairness (mostly for ourselves), but also justice for wrongs committed against us. *Someone needs to pay.* (Forgive? Well, maybe, *if* you ask for my forgiveness, acknowledge what a low-down rotten slime you are, and take the proper punishment. But forgive someone who's not even sorry? No way.)

Yet Someone has already paid for that sin against me. I can forgive the unrepentant, because Jesus took the punishment for *my* sins while I was still a sinner (Romans 5:8).

⮑ Dear sister, do you carry resentment and unforgiveness against someone who has hurt you deeply? Do you hope that person "gets what's coming to them"? Write about it.

_____

_____

_____

_____

_____

_____

_____

_____

From the Word

Do not rejoice when your enemy falls, and do not let your heart be glad when he stumbles; lest the Lord see it, and it displease Him. (Proverbs 24:17–18 NKJV)

And when you stand praying, if you hold anything against anyone, forgive him, *so that* your Father in heaven may forgive you your sins. (Mark 11:25; emphasis added)

Prayer

Ask God for a spirit of forgiveness toward that person who has hurt or offended you. Praise God for His mercy, love, and forgiveness toward you. Thank God that His mercy outweighs His justice.

_____

_____

_____

_____

_____

_____

Yo-Yo snorted. "In case you guys never thought about it, everybody in prison has a name. Maybe you guys—" She checked herself. "Maybe we are s'posed to, you know, pray for her. Or visit her. You know, like Ruth did for me."

"Oh, who's sounding 'spiritual' now?" I snapped. "Ruth wasn't your *victim*. And all you did was forge a couple of checks." I shut my mouth, afraid of the sudden anger that heated my words.

Yo-Yo just shrugged, unperturbed. "All I'm sayin' is, this *is* The Yada Yada *Prayer* Group, ain't it? So . . . pray."

Where did she get off getting so holy all of a sudden? Yo-Yo hadn't been a Christian more than a few months, didn't even go to church yet. What did *she* know? . . .

"Well, now, the way I see it is . . ." Florida jabbed her finger at no one in particular. "I don't like this woman. Wouldn't mind if I never saw her again all my born days. Same time, I didn't like myself five, ten years ago either. And God still saw fit to give me another chance."

—*The Yada Yada Prayer Group Gets Down*, pp. 199–200

Reflection

My father used to wear a button that said: P B P G I N F W M Y— meaning "Please Be Patient; God Is Not Finished With Me Yet." I've still got that button, and it's still true. I'm a work in progress . . . and so are you. I am *so* grateful that God is patient with me. I must be a slow learner, because many of the things I've known all my life are just now becoming manifest in my life—and I'm a grandparent! (A kickin' grandma, but a grandma nonetheless.)

~ Dear sister, in what ways has God been patient with you? How has He given you a second chance? Can you extend that same patience and mercy toward someone who's getting on your last nerve? Someone who has truly wronged you? Can you pray that God would *bless* this person?

_____

_____

_____

_____

_____

From the Word

. . . I tell you: Love your enemies and pray for those who persecute you, that you may be sons of your Father in heaven. . . . If you love those who love you, what reward will you get? Are not even the tax collectors doing that? (Matthew 5:44–46)

Prayer

~ Pray for the person who annoys you the most—in your family, at your job, or at church. (Or all of the above!) Ask God to give you love for this person—and a natural way to express that love. Praise God that He is a God of second chances.

_____

_____

_____

_____

_____

_____

"Don't come crying to me about how bad you feel. What you feel ain't *nothin'* compared to what I'm dealing with right now, and I don't have time to worry about your hurt feelings. Get over it, Jodi—that's all I can say."

A dozen backlashes sprang to my tongue, but I knew I wouldn't say them. . . . I was so mad and so hurt, I wanted to throw pots and pans or break a window or something—anything. Instead I just clenched my fists and my jaw and sputtered, *"Arrrrrggghhhh!"* at the top of my lungs. I paced back and forth between the kitchen and dining room, holding a hundred angry dialogues with Adele in my head, telling her *she's* the one who needs to "get over it" instead of taking it out on friends who never did anything to her. . . .

—*The Yada Yada Prayer Group Gets Down*, p. 221

Reflection

I was a pretty good "dumper" in my early years of marriage, stuffing frustrations and irritations until some careless remark or thoughtless deed brought it all spewing out on my husband's head. He, of course, backed off in bewilderment until I had cooled down. But I had this romantic fantasy that he would reach through my angry outburst and say, "Honey, I can see you're really upset. I'm sorry. What can I do?" (Uh-uh. Didn't happen. *Fantasy* is right.)

But what's to stop me from living out my fantasy when someone's angry with me? To really listen to what's beneath the words? To reach out and say, "I'm sorry. You're hurting. I'm here for you"?

Think about it. What did Jodi miss in what Adele said to her? How was *Adele* hurting?

~ Are you struggling with a relationship or situation in which people are telling you, "Just get over it"? Can you let go of your self-pity and put yourself in the other person's place? What would it mean to forgive this person and "let it go"? Is God asking, "How long are you going to wallow in self-pity?" (See 1 Kings 19.)

_____

_____

_____

_____

From the Word

Why do you . . . complain, O Israel, "My way is hidden from the LORD; my cause is disregarded by my God"? Do you not know? Have you not heard? The LORD is the everlasting God, the Creator of the ends of the earth. He will not grow tired or weary, and his understanding no one can fathom. He gives strength to the weary and increases the power of the weak. (Isaiah 40:27–29)

Prayer

~ Pray for a willingness to end your pity party. Ask God to replace your moping with sensitivity to the hurt in the other person's spirit.

_____

_____

_____

_____

Day 33—*Let That One Go*

I saw my dad peeking in the window of my classroom door just as the dismissal bell rang. Hoping [my parents] wouldn't get run down by the herd of eight-year-olds stampeding for their hard-earned weekend, I called them in, introduced them to my student teacher, and showed them around the now-empty classroom.

My dad stopped by the stove-size, foil-covered box I used as a lost-and-found. "What's a 'Darn Lucky Box'?" I explained that if kids left their things lying around, into the box they went, and the kids were "darn lucky" to get them back—*if* they paid a twenty-five-cent fine.

My mother frowned. "But did you have to say 'darn'?"

I decided to let that one go and hustled them out of the classroom.

—*The Yada Yada Prayer Group Gets Down*, p. 247

Reflection

When I'm invited to a wedding shower and asked to give some advice, I usually say: "There will be times when you feel like yelling hysterically, crying hysterically, or laughing hysterically. Choose laughter." In my own marriage, I have discovered that a sense of humor goes a long way.

The same is true of the family of God. Oh, my, how we can step on each other's toes. The things we criticize each other for! But God's more concerned about injustice, the cry of the poor, and our self-centeredness than He is about a pierced ear or a bare midriff.

🖎 How do you deal with petty sensitivities in other Christians? Feel like lashing back? Can you laugh about it? How hard would it be to "let it go"?

_____

_____

_____

_____

_____

From the Word

Since you died with Christ to the basic principles of this
world, why, as though you still belonged to it, do you submit
to its rules: "Do not handle! Do not taste! Do not touch!"?
These are all destined to perish with use, because they are
based on human commands and teachings. Such regulations
indeed have an appearance of wisdom, with their self-imposed
worship, their false humility and their harsh treatment of the
body, but they lack any value in restraining sensual indulgence.
(Colossians 2:20–23)

Prayer

Pray for the grace not to make mountains out of molehills.
Thank God for His patience with all your little foibles.
Ask God to magnify your sense of humor. At the same
time, pray that your heart would be broken by the things
that break the heart of God.

_____

_____

_____

_____

_____

Day 34—*Whose Anger Is Righteous?*

None of us said much as we left the prison and climbed back into the car. I felt irritated that my mental image of Bandana Woman didn't stand up to the dull-eyed, pathetic creature we'd just left. But I didn't want to feel sorry for her. *Isn't some anger appropriate, God? After all, Hoshi's relationship with her parents is a wreck now, thanks to B. W. If we're going to actually relate to this woman, she needs to face that somehow.* With a twinge of satisfaction, I felt my level of anger—righteous anger, of course—nudge back up a notch.

—*The Yada Yada Prayer Group Gets Down,* p. 283

Reflection

Yeah, I'm pretty good at "righteous anger" too—though if I'm honest, it's usually an excuse to stay angry at someone who's blown it. But what is righteous anger, anyway?

If we simply look at the life of Jesus, His anger was usually reserved for the self-righteous sorts who majored in minors, like tithing their dill and cumin while the poor went hungry. As for the average man or woman who'd "blown it" (the woman caught in adultery, the thief on the cross), He was full of compassion and eagerness to forgive.

All through the Bible, God's righteous anger had a goal: to bring about the redemption of His people. Truly righteous anger should have a redemptive purpose. The righteous anger of Nehemiah resulted in action: to rebuild the wall around Jerusalem. The righteous anger of young David resulted in the courage to face the mockery of Goliath.

So, dear friend, do you have the courage to ask, "Is the anger I feel toward so-and-so righteous anger? Or do I need to forgive so-and-so and set him free?"

_____

_____

_____

_____

_____

_____

_____

_____

From the Word

Be ye angry, and sin not: let not the sun go down upon your wrath: Neither give place to the devil. (Ephesians 4:26–27 KJV)

Prayer

Pray for a new understanding of "righteous anger." Ask God to give you the courage to deal with your anger quickly, "before the sun goes down." Ask God to lift the burden of anger you've been carrying and to give you the freedom that comes with forgiving.

_____

_____

_____

_____

_____

_____

_____

_____

Leave it to God . . . Leave it to God . . .

Avis's admonition followed me the rest of the week. Actually, it helped. I knew I was doing a good job—not perfect, but pretty darn good—teaching those third graders, and if I wasn't, I'd hear about it during staff evaluations. Like Avis said, I just needed to keep doing my job. And, I tried to tell myself, if Hakim's mother didn't want him to get tested, that was her problem.

No! I couldn't accept that. Because even though Hakim was bright, he *was* falling behind. And that wasn't fair to him.

Yet I had a whole classroom of kids to worry about.

—*The Yada Yada Prayer Group Gets Down*, pp. 305–306

Reflection

I used to tease my husband about his "fix-it" mentality. If I shared a problem with him, he'd shift into "fix-it" gear and offer me all kinds of advice—when all I wanted was a sympathetic ear!

To tell the truth, I have a fix-it mentality too. If one of my kids—even as an adult!—has a problem, my mind churns out all kinds of possible solutions. If I get wind of something going wrong at church or among my friends, I feel an urgency to do something about it. It's a hard balance to keep: not slipping into the grandiosity of thinking it's my battle, yet knowing when to "leave it to God" and trust Him with the ragged edges.

∽ What things in your life do you find hard to "leave to God"? How would trusting God to work it out change your attitude? Your actions? Your spirit?

_____

_____

_____

_____

_____

_____

_____

_____

From the Word

Trust in the LORD with all your heart and lean not on your own understanding; in all your ways acknowledge Him, and He shall direct your paths. (Proverbs 3:5–6 NKJV)

Prayer

Pray that your trust in God's loving care for you would deepen. Cover your concerns in constant prayer with the confidence that prayer is "doing something." Praise God that He is fighting your battles in ways beyond your own understanding.

_____

_____

_____

_____

_____

_____

_____

_____

_____

_____

Instinctively, I glanced at my door locks. *Not locked.* I pushed the button at my fingertips. The locks snapped into place with a loud *click.*

The man paused, slowly bent down, and caught my eye through the passenger side window. "That's right," he said loudly through the glass. "Lock your doors! But you really should keep them locked all the time, lady."

Ohmigosh. He heard me lock the doors! To my chagrin, the man pulled out a set of keys, unlocked the door of the four-door sedan parked along the curb, and got in.

Sheesh, Jodi. He was only getting into his parked car. I was so embarrassed that I didn't even notice the light had turned green until horns started to honk behind me. *Oh, God, he probably thinks I locked the doors because he's black and male and wearing dreads.*

—*The Yada Yada Prayer Group Gets Down,* p. 308

Reflection

This really happened to me, and I had to put it into Yada Yada. While I didn't consciously think I was reacting out of fear and prejudice, it was obvious the young man in dreads experienced a message of rejection—simply because of who he was.

I sometimes struggle with feeling rejected. But it made me wonder, *How often do I give messages of rejection to others?* Not wanting to be bothered. Staying safely in my comfort zone. Holding others at arm's length so I don't have to deal with their pain or reality. Hiding my real attitudes, stereotypes, and prejudices behind a mask of politeness.

~ Now consider: Are there folks you don't feel comfortable being around? Why? Do you think your discomfort makes these people feel rejected? What might you do to extend acceptance—the kind of unconditional love and acceptance Jesus has for each of us—to someone outside your comfort zone? (Put a name to that "someone.")

_____

_____

_____

_____

From the Word

Search me, O God, and know my heart; test me and know my anxious thoughts. See if there is any offensive way in me, and lead me in the way everlasting. (Psalm 139:23–24)

Prayer

~ Pray the above verse, asking God to search your heart for anxious thoughts that may be putting a barrier between you and others. Ask God to forgive you for "any offensive way" in you—and the courage to ask others for forgiveness if you have offended them. Thank God for counting you worthy in spite of your weaknesses and failings. Ask God to help you see others as also worthy through His eyes of love.

_____

_____

_____

_____

_____

Day 37—*God's View*

When all our plates had been served, Denny lifted his wine glass to make a toast. "To Adele. May she . . ." He paused, searching for words. "May she 'be anxious for nothing,' 'give thanks in all things,' and experience a 'peace that passes all understanding.' And . . . I do mean that."

We clinked glasses. Then I raised my glass again. "To Adele—noble and kind."

Denny's glass paused in midair. "Noble. And kind." His expression begged for an explanation.

"Well, that's what the name Adele means: noble and kind."

He grunted. "I think she missed her calling."

"Or maybe that's how God thinks of her," Amanda said. Denny and I stared at our daughter as she nonchalantly shoveled in another mouthful of cacciatore.

Out of the mouths of teenagers, Lord . . .

—*The Yada Yada Prayer Group Gets Down*, pp. 335–336

Reflection

Scripture tends to make a big deal of the meaning of names (Isaiah: "God is my helper"; Immanuel: "God with us;" Ruth: "friend of beauty"). My husband's name is David, meaning "beloved." (Gotta love it—grin.) I was named after my grandmother, Aganetha—shortened to "Neta," thank goodness—but I could never find what it meant. However, when my dad called me by *both* my names ("Neta Jean!"), I knew I was in trouble.

Whatever our names, we tend to "live into" the way others see us. If a child is called stupid or dumb or lazy . . . guess what? If a young man or woman is called courageous or determined or smart . . . guess what? (Remember, God sometimes changed a person's name in the biblical story to reflect a change in his or her life.)

The meaning of my name? I discovered it while working on the first Yada Yada novel. I stared at the computer screen: "Neta" means "grace." I couldn't help it. I put my head down on my keyboard . . . and wept.

⁓ Do you know the meaning of your name? What does its meaning *mean* to you? By what name do you think God calls you?

_____

_____

_____

_____

From the Word

"For my thoughts are not your thoughts, neither are your ways my ways," declares the LORD. (Isaiah 55:8)

A Prayer to Share

"O Father! I am so thankful that You see us—this sister using this journal and me—as Your beloved daughters. We are Your creation, and in spite of our faults, our mistakes, the mud of life that splatters our soul, You see us through eyes of love—washed and perfumed and dressed to dance in our garments of praise. Thank You, Lord! We bless Your name!"

⁓ Now, add to the prayer . . .

_____

_____

_____

_____

_____

"You've come a long way, Mark—small-town Georgia to a major university," Stu said.

Mark grinned wryly. "You could say that. First person in my family to go to college, much less get a Ph.D. Grandma and Auntie Bell told me once a day, if not twice, that God put a gift in me, and it'd be a sin not to be the 'somebody' I was created to be. I'll probably never know what they sacrificed to get me there—but you should've seen those two when I got my doctorate. Jumping up and down, weeping and carrying on—though Grandma made it very clear I still had to wipe my feet at the front door and say 'Yes, ma'am' at *her* house."

That got a chuckle from the rest of us. But even as we laughed, I noticed a small frown gather on Mark's face, and he pushed his potatoes around absently. "Then there are days I realize we haven't come very far, after all," he said softly. . . .

"Once I step away from Northwestern's campus, I'm just another black man. Whatever those particular cops think about blacks in general, well, that's what they see."

—*The Yada Yada Prayer Group Gets Down*, pp. 365, 367

Reflection

Yes, we have come a long way in matters of justice. And yes, we still have a long way to go. Our government can legislate laws, but only God can change hearts and minds. Our churches can have all the right doctrines, but only knowing the heart of God can help us embrace the *entire* body of Christ as our brothers and sisters. (Unfortunately, eleven o'clock on Sunday morning is still the most segregated hour of the week.)

For me, it's an ongoing journey: learning to walk like Jesus, talk like Jesus, and live like Jesus. But sometimes all my religious activity gets in the way, when what Jesus really wants is for me to see each person through His eyes—that beloved "somebody" God created each of us to be.

☞   What about you? Do you long to experience the reality of what the body of Christ should be, a house of prayer for all nations? What gets in your way?

_____

_____

_____

_____

From the Word

I hate, I despise your religious feasts; I cannot stand your assemblies. Even though you bring me burnt offerings and grain offerings, I will not accept them. . . . Away with the noise of your songs! I will not listen to the music of your harps. But let justice roll on like a river, righteousness like a never-failing stream! (Amos 5:21–24)

Prayer

☞   Why not pray: "*Oh God, I want Your justice and Your righteousness to live in me. Purge my heart of anything that stands in the way of embracing as my brothers and sisters all those who call You Lord ! I especially pray for new relationships with . . .* "

_____

_____

_____

_____

We left the prison parking lot in silence, a little afraid to break the spell. At least, I was wondering what Becky Wallace was thinking right about now. What had Hoshi's words, "I forgive you," meant to her? Especially since B.W. hadn't actually come out and said, "I'm sorry."

Huh. Not that you've ever fuzzed the edges of an apology, Jodi Baxter. Well, okay, so it was a lot easier to say, *"I didn't mean to"* or *"Guess I messed up."* Saying "I'm sorry" was downright admitting that a wrong had been done, a wrong that needed forgiving. And to be honest, I wasn't very quick on the forgiving end either. Didn't want to let the person who wronged me off the hook *that* easy. . . .

Hoshi kept her head turned toward the window, as if talking to her own reflection. "I could not imagine saying, 'I forgive you.' But when I saw her today . . . it wasn't so hard. Not after she said, 'I'm sorry.'"

I started to say, *"But she didn't, really"*—then realized that Hoshi had given Becky the benefit of the doubt; she had listened beyond her words to her heart.

"Uh-huh," Florida muttered. "It's when they *don't* say 'sorry' that forgivin' gets hard. Still, sometimes ya gotta do it for your own sanity. Maybe that's why Jesus tol' us to forgive our enemies—more for our sake than theirs."

—*The Yada Yada Prayer Group Gets Down,* pp. 381–382

Reflection

The late Lewis B. Smedes wrote a lot about forgiveness. He opened my eyes to the importance of forgiveness, not just for the person who needs forgiving, but also for the person who has been sinned against. In a nutshell, Smedes said, "Do yourself a favor—forgive."

This author helped me understand that if I do not forgive the one who has hurt me, I give that person the power to hurt me again and again and again every time my mind recalls the betrayal, the cutting word, the disloyalty, the violent act. Forgiveness, on the other hand, not only sets the other person free, but it sets *me* free as well.

∾ Dear sister, are you holding on to a hurt that pains your heart each time you think about it? Write it down, give it to God, forgive the person who wronged you—and set yourself free.

_____

_____

_____

_____

From the Word

And when you stand praying, if you hold anything against anyone, forgive him, so that your Father in heaven may forgive you your sins. (Mark 11:25)

Prayer

∾ Pray that God will give you the grace to forgive the person who has hurt you. Thank God for the freedom that forgiveness offers, not only for the offender, but for you as well.

_____

_____

_____

_____

Suddenly I realized what Denny wanted to do, and why. *Jesus gave us the way to break the legacy of sin . . .*

Denny let go of my hand and knelt down beside MaDear's wheelchair. I knelt down with him, kneeling low so that she was looking down on us. "Mrs. . . . ." Denny looked up at Adele, searching for MaDear's real name.

"Skuggs," said Adele. "Sally Skuggs."

"Mrs. Skuggs," Denny continued, his voice husky, "what I did was wrong and evil. You have every right to be angry. But I have come to ask if you could forgive me. I . . . I can't bring your brother back, but I ask you to forgive me for how we white folks wronged your people, and your family in particular."

—*The Yada Yada Prayer Group Gets Down,* p. 397

Reflection

Whoa. Why did Denny repent of a sin he hadn't committed? How fair is that? Yet in the third Yada Yada novel, he tells Jodi that he apologized because MaDear "needed to hear *someone* say, 'I'm sorry.' And because I'm not guilt-free."

On one hand, Denny did a Christlike thing—he took on the sins of another in order to set poor, confused MaDear free in her mind and spirit. On the other hand, Denny realized he, too, needed forgiveness for the underlying sin of racism that has infected our nation. Like Nehemiah (1:4–7), he was asking for forgiveness *on behalf of himself and his own people.*

Why did I write such a scene into this novel? Because of Jesus. There is nothing *fair* about Jesus taking all my sins, all your sins, all the sins of the world on Himself, in order to set us free.

⤸ Write down any questions, thoughts, or feelings that bubble up in you about this concept of asking forgiveness "on behalf of your people."

_____

_____

_____

_____

From the Word

I confess the sins we Israelites, including myself and my father's house, have committed against you. We have acted very wickedly toward you. We have not obeyed the commands, decrees and laws you gave your servant Moses."
(Nehemiah 1:6–7)

Prayer

⤸ Offer up this prayer: *"Precious Lord, since I owed so much, I don't have to worry if someone charges something extra to my account, because You paid it all, Jesus! Search me, oh God, and show me if there are lingering attitudes that need cleansing from my life. Show me if there is anyone who needs to hear 'I'm sorry' from my lips. Specifically . . ."*

_____

_____

_____

_____

_____

_____

Section 3

Redemption

Day 41—*Washed in the Blood*

"Well, now, see?" Florida grinned slyly. "I been prayin' that this here Polar Bear thing be like a prophecy, an' someday we gonna see all these kids come outta that water washed in the blood of Jesus."

Yo-Yo had one leg back in her overalls and one leg out. But she froze in midhop as if someone had yelled "Red light!" in the kids' party game. Her blue-gray eyes widened. "Whatcha talkin' 'bout, Florida? Washed in *what* blood?"

—*The Yada Yada Prayer Group Gets Real*, p. 19

Reflection

I don't hear people talking much about being "washed in the blood of Jesus" these days—not even church folks. Especially not around the sophisticated Starbucks crowd, growing up worldly wise in the new millennium. It sounds so . . . weird. Gruesome. Maybe even cultish. (No wonder Yo-Yo yelped!)

∼ But reflect on that phrase for a few moments. How do you react when you hear about being "washed in the blood of Jesus"? Does it seem like a religious cliché? What do you think it means? Does it mean anything to you?

_____

_____

_____

_____

_____

_____

_____

_____

From the Word

To Him who loved us and washed us from our sins in His own blood, and has made us kings and priests to His God and Father, to Him be glory and dominion forever and ever. Amen. (Revelation 1:5–6 NKJV)

Prayer

Pray that God the Father would reveal the truth to you about what it means to be "washed in the blood" of His Son, Jesus.

_____

_____

_____

_____

_____

_____

_____

_____

_____

_____

_____

_____

_____

_____

_____

_____

_____

_____

_____

Day 42—*"Dull and Boring" Would Be Nice*

[Avis and Jodi are on the phone.] "I'm glad you called, Jodi. It was a tough year but a good year. God gave us the Yada Yada Prayer Group—who would've thought? And we've all learned a lot about God's faithfulness to us in the midst of all the . . . *stuff* that went down."

A feel-sorry-for-myself lump gathered in my throat. "Yeah. I was just telling God I wouldn't mind a few months of 'dull and boring' right about now."

Avis laughed. "I'll stand in agreement with that! Let's all pray for 'dull and boring' . . ."

—*The Yada Yada Prayer Group Gets Real,* p. 28

Reflection

Oh boy, can I relate! In fact, I've been telling God the same thing lately: "I could sure use some 'dull and boring' in my life right now." Or peace and quiet. Or fewer requests to do this or that. Maybe a power outage so the phone would go silent and the computer screen would stay black. Instead, my life just got busier and more complicated! I feel like shaking my fist at God and yelling, "What part of 'dull and boring' don't You understand!"

How about you? Feel too busy? Too many demands on your life? Missing that "quiet time" with God? (Okay, I hear you: *"What* quiet time?! I've got three kids!") Jot down some of the things that feel overwhelming in your life right now. What would a "balanced" life look like for you?

_____

_____

_____

_____

From the Word

Come to me, all you who are weary and burdened, and I will give you rest. Take my yoke upon you and learn from me, for I am gentle and humble in heart, and you will find rest for your souls. For my yoke is easy and my burden is light. (Matthew 11:28–30)

A Prayer for Both of Us

"Oh God, compassionate Father, Your daughters are tired and often overwhelmed. We know that's not the 'rest for your souls' that Jesus promised to those who follow Him. Where did we get off-track? Help us, Lord. Help us learn how to say no when our plate is already full. Help us learn how to rest in You when circumstances are beyond our control. Help our families and all those we interact with each day experience Your peace when they are around us. Fill us with Your peace, even in the middle of all our busyness, worries, and concerns. Thank You that our burdens are light when we let You carry them!"

What would you like to add?

_____

_____

_____

_____

_____

_____

_____

_____

_____

Day 43—*None of Us Is Guilt-Free*

"Jodi?" Nony's low voice seemed meant for my ears only. I leaned closer. "How is Denny—after MaDear's terrible accusation, I mean? While I was in South Africa, seeing the still-painful struggle my country is going through after the end of apartheid . . . I kept thinking about Denny and MaDear, aching for them both. And praying for them, praying for all my brothers and sisters, black and white, weeping for all the hurts still quivering in a million hearts as we take stumbling steps forward—praying that forgiveness and God's love will one day prevail."

A lump gathered in my throat. *Nony doesn't know. . . .* When I had a chance, I'd tell her about Denny's decision to ask MaDear's forgiveness—as though he really had committed that sin against her. *"Because,"* he had explained to me later, *"she needed to hear someone say, 'I'm sorry.' And because I'm not guilt-free."*

—*The Yada Yada Prayer Group Gets Real,* pp. 43, 44

Reflection

When it comes to racial sins in our country, it's so easy to get defensive: "I'm not responsible." "I'm not a bigot." "Don't blame me." This changed for me when I realized that none of us is guilt-free. My private prejudices . . . the ease with which I can ignore the lingering effects of racism and discrimination . . . the privileges I take for granted as part of the majority culture—all add up to a responsibility to own my share of the racial divide still plaguing our neighborhoods, our churches, and our dinner tables. And I've learned how healing it can be for those who are hurting to hear someone say, "I'm sorry for the pain. Sorry for not speaking up. Sorry for not understanding."

What are some of the defenses you feel when it comes to relating to others across race and culture? (Don't worry; you're not alone. I've been there too!) What, if anything, has been helpful to you to lay down those defenses?

_____

_____

_____

_____

_____

From the Word

All of us have become like one who is unclean, and all our righteous acts are like filthy rags; we all shrivel up like a leaf, and like the wind our sins sweep us away. (Isaiah 64:6)

Prayer

Praise God that it is not *our* "righteousness" that saves us, because we can never be good enough. Thank Him for clothing us with *His* righteousness when we are willing to give up our defenses and accept His grace and mercy. Ask God to open your eyes to ways you might help bring about racial healing in your own community. Pray for the healing of our nation, our cities, our neighborhoods, and especially our churches.

_____

_____

_____

_____

_____

Day 44—*Going to the Top*

For some odd reason, the song I'd been listening to in the car the other day popped into my head: *"God is in control."* Did I believe that? Or was I always going to approach problems the Old Jodi way—stewing and fretting till I'd wrestled them to the ground? No! My Yada Yada sisters had been teaching me to "go to the top" on the first round, not the last. Not just to believe in God, but to *believe* God.

"Denny, why don't we pray about it and ask God what we should do?" And then I giggled. "Good grief. I sound just like my dad. I used to *hate* it when he said that!"

—*The Yada Yada Prayer Group Gets Real*, pp. 50–51

Reflection

As a teenager, I used to get annoyed when I'd come to my dad with a problem, and he'd say, "Let's pray about it." Pray? He was my dad! He was supposed to have answers! Prayer seemed like a cop-out. *(Ha. Dad doesn't have an answer, so he's covering up by sounding pious.)*

What I didn't understand till many years later was that my dad was trying to bring me to the Source of all wisdom, all power, all love. How much grief I would have saved myself if I'd learned at an earlier age to seek God's wisdom, if I'd truly believed that God was in control of my life, if I'd truly trusted His promises.

~ Dear sister, maybe like me you have believed *in* God for a long time. But do you *believe* God? (Reread the Reflection on Day 10 for more about the difference between believing *in* God versus *believing God*.) Do you really believe God's promises are for you? What does your heart say?

_____

_____

_____

_____

_____

_____

_____

_____

From the Word

If any of you lacks wisdom, he should ask God, who gives generously to all without finding fault, and it will be given to him. (James 1:5)

Prayer

Pray *first.* What is troubling your spirit today? Do you need wisdom? Have you taken your request to Jesus yet? (The very fact that you're using this prayer journal is a good sign that prayer *is* an important part of your life—or you want it to be.) Ask God to make known His wisdom in your life and in this situation.

_____

_____

_____

_____

_____

_____

_____

_____

_____

Day 45—*Hitting the Ceiling*

My insides kind of collapsed. "Why didn't you just *tell* us? Sheesh—all the stuff people said . . ."

Avis shook her head. "Didn't trust myself. I can get very angry about it. And to tell you the truth, Jodi, I'm tired of praying about it. I've prayed and prayed for years that justice would be done, that someone would tell the truth, but it's like all my prayers hit the ceiling. *Bam, bam!* They fall back flat on my face."

My jaw nearly dropped. I wasn't sure I'd heard right. Avis was always encouraging the rest of us to "press on through" in prayer, regardless of the circumstances.

—The Yada Yada Prayer Group Gets Real, p. 78

Reflection

"All my prayers hit the ceiling" . . . I've felt like that. Tired of God's silence. Frustrated that my faith or my prayers don't seem to be moving any mountains.

I have a particular situation in my life over which I've prayed, I've wept, I've fasted . . . but so far God hasn't answered my prayer—at least, not in the way I was hoping for. And I've wondered, what does it *mean* to pray "in His name" or "according to His will"? Seems too easy to just say, "In Jesus' name, amen" or, "Thy will be done." Recently I've changed my prayer to simply, "Lord, work out Your purpose in this situation." I no longer pretend to know what that is and have quit telling God what I think He should do. Yet I do still believe God wants me to pray.

Take a moment to reflect on a situation in which you feel like your prayers are "hitting the ceiling." What do you think it means to pray in the name of Jesus or to pray according to His will?

_____

_____

_____

_____

_____

_____

From the Word

This is the confidence we have in approaching God: that if
we ask anything according to his will, he hears us. And if we
know that he hears us—whatever we ask—we know that we
have what we asked of him. (1 John 5:14–15)

Prayer

Pray once more for that person or situation in which it feels
like your prayers are "hitting the ceiling." (After all, it is
God's job to answer and our job to pray.)

_____

_____

_____

_____

_____

_____

_____

_____

_____

_____

Day 46—*Worry . . . or Pray*

A soft rumble beside me told me Denny was out. Gone.

I slid out of his embrace but lay awake for a while, worried about Delores . . . worried about Florida . . . and Carla . . . and Carl . . . and Chris. . . . I realized I'd practically committed myself to this *quinceañera* thing for Amanda . . . and Stu was moving in on Saturday—really, truly moving into my house! Well, upstairs, but still . . .

I could feel my own heartbeat pick up a little. If I wasn't careful, I could work myself into a stew and lose half a night's sleep. Or I could pray. Pray instead of worry—well, *that* was sure enough biblical! But I was tired of my "Be with Delores, bless Florida, take care of Carla" prayers. Maybe I could pray some Scripture, like Nony did so often.

—*The Yada Yada Prayer Group Gets Real,* pp. 109–110

Reflection

It's hard not to worry. If you're a parent, you *always* worry about your kids, even when they're grown and away from home. And then there's money and job stress and relationships gone sour . . . the list can be endless!

But you and I know that stewing and fretting accomplishes nothing. (So why do we do it anyway? Duh!) I'm trying to learn how to turn my worry into prayers that focus on God's promises —and the most helpful way I've found is to actually "pray" the Scriptures, personalizing various prayers that Jesus and other biblical writers prayed.

✎ Dear sister, what are the worries and concerns that weigh down your heart right now? It helps to name them, so write them down.

_____

_____

_____

_____

_____

_____

From the Word

Rejoice in the Lord always. I will say it again: Rejoice! Let
your gentleness be evident to all. The Lord is near. Do not be
anxious about anything, but in everything, by prayer and
petition, with thanksgiving, present your requests to God.
And the peace of God, which transcends all understanding,
will guard your hearts and your minds in Christ Jesus.
(Philippians 4:4–7)

Prayer

Pray for the person you worry about by personalizing one of
Paul's prayers in the following passages: Ephesians 1:15–19;
Ephesians 3:14–21; Philippians 1:9–11; or Colossians
1:9–12. Write out that prayer here.

_____

_____

_____

_____

_____

_____

_____

... I pulled open the freezer door and assessed the situation: a package of chicken thighs, leftover potatoes au gratin, and a skinned catfish Denny "caught" at Dominick's on sale. None of it looked interesting; all of it looked like work—except the potatoes. What I wouldn't give for big bucks to take the whole family out for dinner every Friday!

Chanda can—every day if she wants to.

Whoa. Where did *that* renegade thought come from? I certainly wasn't jealous of Chanda—was I? Maybe Chanda's [lottery] winnings. It was just too easy; it didn't seem fair. . . . Denny and I played by all the rules—got married, *then* had kids, worked two jobs, paid off all our school loans, tithed to the church, paid our bills, didn't waste our money on the lottery or foolish schemes—and yet we never really got ahead. The budget noose was just as tight today as twenty years ago.

—*The Yada Yada Prayer Group Gets Real,* p. 133

Reflection

I was *sure* I wasn't the jealous type—till that booksellers' convention where I saw other authors signing stacks of books for long lines of fans, big-name authors being chased for interviews, and editors and authors alike heading back to the Hilton or the Embassy Suites or the Omni Hotel after a long day. My husband and I, on the other hand, had no book signings, no interviews (even though we had several books in print that year), and we were staying in a budget motel with peeling wallpaper.

I had to admit it: I was jealous. But I didn't like what it was doing to my spirit. Self-centered. Unsatisfied. Petty. Where were my thanks and praise?

❧ Let's be honest. Life *isn't* fair. You play by the rules, but the other guy gets the promotion. You work two jobs to support your family, but your neighbor has a new Lexus while you're still driving a car from the last century (literally). Can you identify feelings of jealousy, envy, or resentment that are eating away at your contentment?

_____

_____

_____

_____

From the Word

But godliness with contentment is great gain. For we brought nothing into the world, and we can take nothing out of it. But if we have food and clothing, we will be content with that. People who want to get rich fall into temptation and a trap and into many foolish and harmful desires that plunge men into ruin and destruction. For the love of money is a root of all kinds of evil. (1 Timothy 6:6–10)

Prayer

❧ Give thanks that God isn't fair! (Or we would all be paying for our sins in hell.) Ask God to open your eyes to all the good gifts He has poured into your life. Thank Him! Praise Him! Jump for joy!

_____

_____

_____

_____

Day 48—*A Reminder to Pray*

The bubbles of my bath were fading away, and I saw the scars on my body from the surgery to remove my damaged spleen, and the rod they'd inserted into my left thigh. Scars . . . would they eventually fade? Or always remain as a reminder—

A reminder of what? Of my stupid anger, my failure to be the kind of Christian I thought I was? A constant reminder of the boy who died in front of my car?

A reminder of My grace, Jodi. And a reminder to pray.

Pray?

Yes, pray. I have forgiven you; remember that. You sometimes forget. But the scars can remind you to pray for Jamal's mother, who is still grieving and confused. And for Hakim. Because I put him in your classroom for a reason.

—*The Yada Yada Prayer Group Gets Real*, p. 138

Reflection

I have scars. Do you? One on my leg from an encounter with a strand of loose barbed wire while "riding fence" with my uncle when I was a kid. (I'm kinda proud of that one.) One on my hand from sticking a dishtowel *and* my hand inside a drinking glass that proceeded to burst. (That one is more embarrassing.) And one on my forehead from a car accident when I was driving, an accident in which my father died.

But not all scars are physical. Some scars are like my journal entries of that happy trip preceding the car accident, entries that end abruptly . . . the wedding picture in my photo album of a marriage now broken . . . a memory of a cutting word.

◈ What are some of the "scars" you carry? As you list those scars below, consider that maybe, like Jodi, your scars can serve as reminders to pray—for memories not yet healed, for relationships not yet mended, and for eyes to see God's loving care even in the midst of pain.

_____

_____

_____

_____

From the Word

[Jesus] himself bore our sins in his body on the tree. . . . by his wounds you have been healed. (1 Peter 2:24)

Prayer

◈ Praise God for the wounds He suffered to bring us redemption! Pray that God would continue to bring redemption out of the scars of your life. Pray especially for eyes to see God's loving grace in the middle of your pain.

_____

_____

_____

_____

_____

_____

_____

_____

The wind was kicking up as we got back in the minivan with four coffees-to-go, and the clouds looked heavy, like a big belly about to pop. "Say a prayer, sisters," I muttered. "I really don't want to drive in a snowstorm."

I meant just sending up the silent kind, but Florida—who had taken over the front passenger seat—belted out, "Okay, Lord, You heard my sister here. She don't need ta be drivin' in no snowstorm today, 'cause we all wantin' to get home safe to our families. You're a big God, and we know this is nothin' for You. Just hold off on the snow, all right?"

Well, amen. Sure hoped God didn't mind being bossed around by Florida.

—*The Yada Yada Prayer Group Gets Real,* pp. 155-156

Reflection

Last night I mentioned to a friend at church something that was weighing me down and asked her to pray—and she immediately took my hand and began praying aloud right then. Once that would have startled me, but it is becoming the new pattern of my life. If someone calls me with a prayer request, I ask if I can pray right there on the phone, even if she's at the office. Or I'll pray on the spot with someone in a restaurant, in a car, or on the sidewalk. What a treasure it is to be able to go directly to God—at any time, with anything, with anyone! Not just *saying* I'm going to pray, but *praying*—now!

❧   Would you feel comfortable being prayed for—or praying for someone—aloud, on the spot? Or do you prefer a particular "prayer time" when you can be alone with God? Reflect on the benefits of each.

_____
_____
_____
_____
_____
_____
_____
_____

From the Word

Let us then approach the throne of grace with confidence, so
that we may receive mercy and find grace to help us in our
time of need. (Hebrews 4:16)

Prayer

- Pray with thanksgiving that God has given you access to
His throne room, where you can bring your praise, your
worship, and your petitions—and that you can come any
time, day or night, bad hair day or looking fine, feeling
snarly or on top of the world, alone or with someone by the
hand.

_____
_____
_____
_____
_____
_____

Hoshi nodded thoughtfully. After ten months of Yada Yada, she was still the quietest one among us. She had not wanted to visit Becky Wallace at first—who could blame her!—then surprised all of us by going to the prison a few months ago and telling Becky Wallace that she forgave her. The petition on B. W.'s behalf [to release her on early parole] had actually been Hoshi's idea, but I could sure understand if she was having second thoughts.

"For the last two weeks, I am thinking about sending this petition." Hoshi's voice was surprisingly assertive. "I don't know about 'is she ready.' Maybe that is for the parole board to decide? But what Yo-Yo said is true—this is just as much about us. In Asian culture, we do not focus just on the individual, but on the responsibility of the whole community. So I've been asking myself: Have I really forgiven her? How far does that forgiveness go? What role does my forgiveness—our forgiveness—play in redeeming this woman to once again be part of the community?"

How far does that forgiveness go?

—*The Yada Yada Prayer Group Gets Real*, p. 218–219

Reflection

I'll never forget seeing the stage play of Victor Hugo's novel *Les Misérables*. In one powerful scene, a bitter and desperate Valjean, only recently released from prison for stealing a loaf of bread, is caught with the family silver he stole from the good bishop's house—only to have the bishop say, "I'm delighted to see you! Have you forgotten that I gave you the candlesticks as well?" Dismissing the bewildered policemen, the bishop sends Valjean off with enough valuable silver to begin a new life, only saying to him,

"Do not forget, do not ever forget, that you have promised me to use the money to make yourself an honest man." Valjean is transformed by the bishop's sacrificial forgiveness, dedicating himself to helping others in need, and . . . well, you know the rest of the story.

~ How has Christ's forgiveness changed *your* life? How might your forgiveness set another person free? *How far does that forgiveness go?*

_____

_____

_____

_____

From the Word

It is for freedom that Christ has set us free. . . . You, my brothers [and sisters], were called to be free. But do not use your freedom to indulge the sinful nature; rather, serve one another in love. The entire law is summed up in a single command: "Love your neighbor as yourself." (Galatians 5:1, 13–14)

Prayer

~ Bless the name of Jesus that He has forgiven your sins and given you life—not only eternal life with God, but abundant life here and now. Ask God to fill you so full of gratitude that forgiveness spills out of you to free others.

_____

_____

_____

_____

Day 51—*Kinsman Redeemer*

"Denny?" I snuggled closer under the curve of his arm. . . . "What do you really think about testifying at Becky Wallace's parole hearing tomorrow?"

"Funny you should ask. . . . Remember Pastor Clark's sermon on the story of Ruth a couple Sundays ago? . . . I was thinking about Boaz, the 'kinsman redeemer.' . . . If he hadn't taken action, Ruth would have remained a foreigner, an outcast, a childless widow, just marking time and space . . ."

I leaned away from Denny's arm and twisted so I could look at him. I almost blurted, *"We're not 'kinsmen' to Becky Wallace!"* But in a flash of understanding, I knew what he was trying to say. Becky Wallace had dropped into our lives—kind of like Ruth and Naomi dropping back into Boaz's life after years in a "far country"—and we had a choice: we could do nothing and let consequences take their natural course, or we could act as her "kinsmen redeemers," helping her to build a new life. At least give it a try.

I shivered. Or shuddered.

—*The Yada Yada Prayer Group Gets Real,* pp. 270–271

Reflection

As mentioned on Day 28, the story of Becky Wallace is a fictionalized version of a true incident. My husband, Dave, and a few others in our church visited Patricia (her real name) while she was in prison. After she served five years, Dave testified at her first parole hearing, saying we had seen much change in her and would welcome her return to Evanston. The board granted her parole but banned her from the state of Illinois for another five years.

Nevertheless, we maintained contact and were delighted when Patricia wrote to us, saying she had given her heart to Jesus, largely because of the Christian love she had received in prison. Not long after that we received an announcement of her marriage to a Christian man. God has also given Patricia a powerful prison ministry to women because of her testimony.

✎   Has God dropped someone into your life—unasked, unannounced, and maybe unwelcome? What feelings do you have about this person? Are you willing to consider whether God has a redemptive purpose in mind?

_____

_____

_____

_____

From the Word

He redeemed us in order that the blessing given to Abraham might come to the Gentiles through Christ Jesus, so that by faith we might receive the promise of the Spirit. (Galatians 3:14)

Prayer

✎   Pray for the person you mentioned above. Ask God to show you His reason for bringing this person into your life.

_____

_____

_____

_____

_____

_____

_____

Day 52—*Have You Died Yet?*

It took a second or two for Stu's words to compute, but when they did, I yelped. "*What?!* Becky Wallace live *here?!* You're out of your mind, Leslie Stuart!"

Stu shrugged. "Why? Didn't Jesus say if we have two coats we should give one to the guy who has none? I've got three bedrooms. Becky has none. Same thing."

It is NOT! I wanted to scream. But I was dangerously close to losing it, and I clamped my teeth, knowing I needed time to cool down. But my mind still raged. *Becky Wallace in my house? After what she did here? Over my dead body.*

—*The Yada Yada Prayer Group Gets Real,* p. 285

Reflection

"Over my dead body." Funny how noble it sounds in Scripture to "lay down your life for your friends"—until it requires dying to self in real life. Sure, I like to think of myself as a noble, sacrificial person . . . as long as it doesn't really cost me anything.

- Has God asked something of you lately—via your spouse, your boss, or even your kids—that would require you to die to yourself? Does it feel like someone is taking advantage of you? What would happen if you gave yourself sacrificially in this situation? (I do not mean to imply that you are automatically required to do *everything* someone asks of you. All I'm saying is to consider what it means to "lay down your life for your friends" on a practical, day-to-day level.)

____

____

____

____

_____

_____

_____

_____

_____

_____

_____

_____

_____

From the Word

Greater love has no one than this, that he lay down his life
for his friends. (John 15:13)

Prayer

Pray for the courage to live sacrificially, with the kind of
love for others that Christ Jesus has for you. Ask God for
wisdom in the specific situation you face that feels like
"dying to self."

_____

_____

_____

_____

_____

_____

_____

_____

_____

_____

"I couldn't prove I'd been date raped, couldn't face telling my family, couldn't bear raising a child alone. I'd seen too many single moms trapped, struggling, ending up on welfare. And I . . . I was embarrassed. I was thirty-two, for heaven's sake! I've got a masters' degree! How could I let this happen to me? I'm smart, I'm educated, I'm supposed to be helping people who make dumb mistakes!" Stu's eyes glittered for a brief moment, and then her shoulders slumped. "So I . . . I told myself I had no choice. But I cried for days. Everyone wondered what was wrong. To cope, I . . . I shut everybody who knew me out of my life. Distanced myself from my family, stopped going to St. John's, quit my DCFS job, took a real-estate course, moved, started a new life. Put it out of my mind. Proved to myself I could survive one mistake and start over. But . . ."

—*The Yada Yada Prayer Group Gets Real*, p. 303

Reflection

No choice? Yes, Satan would like us to believe that—whether it is about an unwanted pregnancy or any other situation in which we feel backed into a corner. Oh, sister, sometimes you and I feel so alone in a struggle—but we are not alone!

First of all, God says He will *never* leave us or forsake us (Deuteronomy 31:6–8—also notice how many times Joshua was told to "be strong and courageous"!). And *nothing* that happens to us can separate us from the love of God (Romans 8:35–39—and notice verse 37, which says we are "more than conquerors"!).

Second, many others have faced a similar struggle—all the way from biblical times up to the present day—and discovered the faithfulness of God. (Mary had an unplanned and unmarried pregnancy, Mary Magdalene was tormented by seven demons, Ruth

was widowed at a young age, Sarah was childless, Esther was
forced to become a trophy bride . . . and on and on the list goes.)

∼ Dear sister, do you face a situation in which you feel all
alone? Pour it out to the One who loves you *so much* that
He put His life on the line for you. Ask Him to give you a
friend—or several friends—to walk this difficult path with
you.

_____

_____

_____

_____

_____

From the Word

No temptation has seized you except what is common to man.
And God is faithful; he will not let you be tempted beyond
what you can bear. But when you are tempted, he will also provide a way out so that you can stand up under it. Therefore, my
dear friends, flee from idolatry. (1 Corinthians 10:13–14)

Prayer

∼ Pray the promises in Romans 8:35–39, making them personal to you and your situation.

_____

_____

_____

_____

_____

Day 54—*Thanking God in Advance*

Lord Jesus! I sent up a quick prayer. *Pour some grace on that conversation.* Wasn't sure what Stu intended to say [to Chanda], but hopefully it would be oil on the troubled waters stirred up the last time those two had talked. Had to admire Stu taking the initiative before we all tried worshipping together. *Thank You in advance, Lord, for what You're going to do.* I smiled to myself. Definitely a New Jodi prayer.

—*The Yada Yada Prayer Group Gets Real,* p. 327

Reflection

Thanking God *before* He answers? Definitely a "New Neta" prayer too! For many years I was pretty much stuck on " . . . but Thy will be done." ("Well, God, this is what I'm asking, but of course I want Your will, not my will," which pretty much covered the bases no matter what happened!). But I've been learning that praise and worship are powerful spiritual weapons, proclaiming Who has the power. When I thank God even before seeing the answers to my prayers, I am saying I believe His promises—even though the circumstances might tell me otherwise.

I was always troubled by that "thank God in all things" bit too. I mean, thank God for the accident in which my dad died? Thank God for the cutting words from one of my best friends? *Get real, God!* Then someone told me—duh!—that it's not thanking God *for* all circumstances, but *in* all circumstances. Oh!

~ Sister, what are the requests on your heart today? They might be big, they might be small, but God cares about them all. Go ahead, list them right here.

_____

_____

_____
_____
_____
_____
_____
_____
_____

From the Word

[Abraham] did not waver at the promise of God through
unbelief, but was strengthened in faith, giving glory to God,
and being fully convinced that what He had promised He
was also able to perform. And therefore "it was accounted to
him for righteousness." (Romans 4:20–22 NKJV)

Prayer

Pray about the needs on your heart, one by one, then thank
God that He is faithful to fulfill His promises . . . that He is
an "on-time" God . . . that His love never fails you . . . that
His purposes are for your good . . . and that the battle is
His, not yours.

_____
_____
_____
_____
_____
_____
_____

Day 55—*Courage to Be Set Free*

I sat quietly in the car for several moments, my door wide open, thinking about the sin that continued to dog me, even though I had confessed to God, confessed to my husband and family, confessed to Yada Yada, been loved and forgiven. But I still didn't feel free. I'd said I was "sorry" to Jamal's mother that day in the courtroom—but how did she hear it? That I was sorry it had happened? Sorry she'd lost her son? Sure. Anybody would be. But had I ever really *confessed my sin* to the mother of the boy I'd killed? Could she ever really forgive me if I didn't?

I wanted to be free. What was it Jesus said? *"If you abide in My Word, you will know the truth, and the truth will set you free."*

I blinked back tears. "God wants to set us free, Stu. With the truth. Listen to God's whisper in your heart. You'll know what's right to say . . . or do."

Right, Jodi. You know what's right to do. But do you have the courage to do it?

—*The Yada Yada Prayer Group Gets Real,* p. 341

Reflection

It's hard to admit I'm wrong. I want to defend myself, explain all the circumstances, cast myself in the best light, and call it a mistake or a misunderstanding. Yet what I really need is the freedom of being forgiven. No excuses. No defensiveness. Just the courage to confess my sin, take responsibility for my part of the problem, and let God take care of all the rest. After all, He has promised to be my shield, my hiding place, and my deliverer (Psalm 18:2)!

✎   My sister, are you feeling weighed down with an unresolved situation or relationship? Maybe it's just a little thing, hardly worth the bother—but it still bothers you. Maybe it's complicated, and you hesitate to take responsibility for your part for fear that will let the others off the hook. Maybe it's decades of hurt family feelings. Whatever it is—and have the courage to write it down here—trust God to be your shield and defender.

_____

_____

_____

_____

_____

From the Word

Confess your sins to each other and pray for each other so that you may be healed. The earnest prayer of a righteous person has great power and wonderful results. (James 5:16 NLT)

Prayer

Pray for the courage to confess your sin to the person who feels wronged. Praise God that He longs for you to be healed and whole—your body, your mind, your soul, and your spirit. Ask God to be your shield and defender when you make yourself vulnerable.

_____

_____

_____

_____

_____

Hakim's mother held up her hand to stop me. Her eyes were dry but bright. "You have had your say. Now let me have mine." She stood and walked over to Hakim's desk, her finger slowly tracing the jagged scar he had dug into the wood with a paper clip. Then she turned back to me.

"I don't know if I can forgive you for killing my son," she said slowly. *(Oh God! To hear her say it like that—"for killing my son"—I can't bear it!)* "I don't know if I'm strong enough to do that. But I have something to say to you too—something I've had to face, even though I haven't wanted to. That day, the day of the accident, Jamal was running against the light, against traffic, with a jacket over his head in a downpour that kept drivers from seeing him. His cousins admit it; the other driver —the one that hit your car—said so too. I couldn't hear it; I wanted to put it all on your head." She took a deep breath. "But my Jamal was also responsible for what happened that day. Not just you."

—*The Yada Yada Prayer Group Gets Real*, p. 372–373

Reflection

In this scene from *The Yada Yada Prayer Group Gets Real*, the Holy Spirit convicted Geraldine of the truth in a way that no amount of argument from Jodi could have done. In fact, Geraldine couldn't have heard it from Jodi. The truth needed to come from within her own spirit. Jesus, *He* made a way.

I'll never forget my six-foot high school senior saying, "You can't *make* me obey you. I obey you because I *choose* to obey you, because I respect you." And he was right. Praise God, respect for us as parents won out over his disagreement with our rules! But his obedience was all the more true, because his choice to obey came from within.

✍ Do you need to trust the work of the Holy Spirit in another person's life? An unbelieving husband, an erring teen, a critical boss, a friend who misunderstands? Can you let go and let God work it out?

_____

_____

_____

_____

From the Word

[Jesus said] But I tell you the truth: It is for your good that I am going away. Unless I go away, the Counselor [Holy Spirit] will not come to you; but if I go, I will send him to you. When he comes, he will convict the world of guilt in regard to sin and righteousness and judgment. (John 16:7–8)

Prayer

✍ Pray for God to help you let go of the need to defend yourself or make something happen, and to trust the Holy Spirit to do the work in another person's life. Be faithful to pray for God's best for this person, for His purposes to be accomplished in his or her life. Ask for God's peace in your own spirit while you wait.

_____

_____

_____

_____

_____

_____

"Well, I got somethin' to shout about," Florida announced. "Peter Douglass—bless that man! Oh, hallelujah!—he done offered a job to my Carl as his mailroom supervisor." The room erupted with shouts of glee. "Wait, wait, that ain't all! He gets two weeks' job training, room for advancement, and—oh, Jesus! Don't know if I can stand it!—full benefits!" Florida was on her feet, waving her hand in the air. *"Thank* ya! Thank ya, Jesus!"

Carl with a job? With benefits? We'd been praying for months—why was I so surprised? Did I have so little faith? Or had I just pegged Carl as "permanently jobless"?

Florida sat down again, fanning herself with her hand. "You gotta pray for me I don't nag him 'bout this job, though. So afraid he gonna do somethin' dumb and lose it. But job training starts tomorrow, so we'll see."

—*The Yada Yada Prayer Group Gets Real,* p. 382

Reflection

Why are we so surprised when God answers our prayers—beyond what we are even asking? Last weekend I was speaking at a women's retreat, and a dear sister asked my ministry partner and me to pray for the healing of her shoulder. She'd been experiencing great pain for weeks. Well, I don't have a lot of experience praying for healing, but obedient to the Scripture, I anointed her shoulder with oil and we prayed. And God loosened up that shoulder right in front of our eyes. That night she slept without pain for the first time in months. The next day she did "windmills" with that arm! I thought, *Whoa, God! Let me get out of Your way. You are so good!*

☞ Take a few minutes to reflect on the past several weeks. Has God answered some of your prayers? Has He been good to you—in ways you weren't even expecting, didn't even pray about, or maybe didn't even notice? Jot them down here.

_____

_____

_____

_____

From the Word

"For I know the plans I have for you," declares the LORD, "plans to prosper you and not to harm you, plans to give you hope and a future. Then you will call upon me and come and pray to me, and I will listen to you. You will seek me and find me when you seek me with all your heart." (Jeremiah 29:11–13)

Prayer

☞ Pray with a thankful heart for the goodness of the Lord. Ask God to open your eyes to all the ways He blesses you each day, ways you may take for granted. Ask God to deepen your trust in His plans "to prosper you and not to harm you." Thank Him that when you seek Him, He is there, waiting and eager to give you "hope and a future."

_____

_____

_____

_____

_____

Armed with a long shovel, Becky tackled the weed-choked flowerbeds with the determination of a prisoner-of-war digging an escape tunnel. Willie Wonka seemed fascinated by all the activity and settled on his haunches nearby like a sidewalk supervisor. It took a gulp of faith for me to go about my business inside the house and leave my dog outside with the same woman who'd threatened to "cut him" during the robbery.

Okay, Jesus, I know I'm a little anxious, and I'm probably being silly. I chopped vegetables for a pot of soup with unnecessary vigor. *But we could use a few guardian angels on the job, if You don't mind. One for Willie Wonka too.* I stepped over to the back door and watched Becky working up a good sweat with the shovel. Only God knew what was going on in her mind and her spirit these days. Maybe *she* was anxious about *us.*

And a guardian angel for Becky too, I added.

—*The Yada Yada Prayer Group Gets Real,* p. 388

Reflection

When my daughter was little, I framed a picture of a guardian angel watching over two little children crossing a footbridge, and I hung it over her bed. That same picture hangs on the wall of my granddaughter's bedroom. I do believe in angels—they play a big role in the Bible!—but we need to be careful not to exalt angels over God. (Angels are popular in the public media right now—a lot more popular than God is!)

Angels are created beings like we are, and they have a special role as God's messengers, spiritual warriors, and guardians. Though we cannot see them, guardian angels are another expression of God's great love for us.

 ∾ What are some of your thoughts about angels? Have you
ever had an experience that made you think, *My guardian
angel must have been looking out for me?*

_____

_____

_____

_____

From the Word

For the angel of the LORD guards all who fear him, and he
rescues them. Taste and see that the LORD is good. Oh, the
joys of those who trust in him! (Psalm 34:7–8 NLT)

Beware that you don't despise a single one of these little ones.
For I tell you that in heaven their angels are always in the
presence of my heavenly Father. (Matthew 18:10 NLT)

Prayer

 ∾ Thank God for His great love for you, even assigning
angels to protect you! Thank Him for His protection
today—all the accidents that *didn't* happen. Give all the
glory to God.

_____

_____

_____

_____

_____

_____

_____

. . . The Garfields arrived with Yo-Yo and her two brothers trailing behind them . . . and I wanted to burst out laughing.

Yo-Yo was wearing a brand-new pair of lavender overalls.

"The name of the Lord is a strong tower," Pastor Clark boomed, covering my giggle that escaped. "The righteous run into it and are safe." Then the praise team launched into the Don Moen worship song based on that same verse: "The name of the Lord is . . . a strong tower!"

The name of the Lord is a strong tower! What a wonderful theme for Avis's wedding and Yo-Yo's baptism. I'd been thinking of the meaning of Avis's name—"Refuge in battle"—as who *she* was to me and to Yada Yada. But a deeper meaning probably went right along with this proverb: Avis herself took refuge in "the name of the Lord," which probably accounted for her peaceful heart and spirit of praise.

—*The Yada Yada Prayer Group Gets Real*, pp. 392–393

Reflection

As I already mentioned in this journal, I enjoyed exploring the meaning of the names of my characters in the Yada Yada novels. At the same time, I feel like a beginner in understanding and appreciating the names of God and their meanings as keys to His attributes and His character. Here are just a few:

El Roi—"The God Who Sees Me"
El Shaddai— "The All-Sufficient One"
Jehovah— "I Am"
Jehovah-Jireh— "The Lord Will Provide"
Jehovah-Rapha— "The Lord Who Heals"
Jehovah-Shalom— "The Lord Is Peace"

🙾   Which names of God are most meaningful to you at this period of your life? Why? Which names (attributes) of God would you like to deepen in your understanding?

_____

_____

_____

_____

_____

From the Word

Hear my cry, O God; listen to my prayer. From the ends of the earth I call to you, I call as my heart grows faint; lead me to the rock that is higher than I. For you have been my refuge, a strong tower against the foe. (Psalm 61:1–3)

The name of the LORD is a strong tower; the righteous run to it and are safe. (Proverbs 18:10)

Prayer

🙾   Pray for greater understanding of the names of God and what they mean—about Who God is and His relationship with you. Praise Him that you can ask anything "in His name"! Thank God that His name is your refuge, the solid rock you cling to. Praise Him for being your provider, your healer, your peace . . .

_____

_____

_____

_____

"Wait!" someone shouted. I was startled to see Becky Wallace pull away from Stu's side and head for the water. At the water's edge, she kicked off her shoes and waded in, heading toward the shivering Yo-Yo. The singing died away as everyone gaped. *What in the world?*

For a nanosecond, I wondered if Becky had figured out a good escape—just head into the water and keep swimming. Or drown the ankle monitor. But she stopped as she met up with Pastor Clark, Denny, and Yo-Yo, saying something and gesturing with her hands. She and Pastor Clark talked intensely for a few minutes. Then the two men looked at each other, and I saw Denny nod.

All four of them turned around and headed back into waist-deep water.

Several of us realized what was happening all at once. *Becky Wallace wanted to be baptized!* Chanda began jumping up and down. "Hallelujah! Hallelujah! Oh, Jesus!" I heard "Glory!" and "Thank You, Jesus!" But Stu caught my eye, and without saying a word, we both kicked off our shoes and waded into the water. That sister needed some sisters around her while she did the bravest thing I'd ever seen. . . .

—*The Yada Yada Prayer Group Gets Real,* pp. 400–401

Reflection

Last Sunday we had a baptism. Our church doesn't have a "baptistry," so we all piled into our cars and drove to the shore of Lake Michigan several blocks away. The day was beautiful for late September—cloudless, warm, the water temperature mild (well, mild for Lake Michigan). Six teenagers and two adults had requested baptism, going public in front of their families, friends, church members—and the startled sunbathers and dog walkers at the lakefront—that Jesus had washed their sins in His blood and declaring themselves "Christ followers." What joy on the beach! What joy in heaven!

⌇ Precious sister, have you been baptized by "the Spirit, the water, and the blood"? If so, write what your baptism means to you. If not, read 1 John 5:6–15 and ask yourself if this is the day that you accept God's gift of eternal life—letting the blood of Jesus Christ cover all your sins, and beginning an awesome journey of life with Jesus.

_____

_____

_____

_____

From the Word

Peter replied, "Repent and be baptized, every one of you, in the name of Jesus Christ for the forgiveness of your sins. And you will receive the gift of the Holy Spirit. The promise is for you and your children and for all who are far off—for all whom the Lord our God will call." (Acts 2:38–39)

Prayer

⌇ Pray with joy! Thank God that Jesus "paid it all" for your sins and mine.

_____

_____

_____

_____

Find out how the
Yada Yada Story begins . . .

I almost didn't go to the Chicago Women's Conference—after all, being thrown together with 500 strangers wasn't exactly my "comfort zone." But I would be rooming with my boss, Avis, and I hoped that I might make a friend or two.

When Avis and I were assigned to a prayer group of 12 women, I wasn't sure what to think. There was Flo, an out-spoken ex-drug addict; Ruth, a Messianic Jew who could smother-mother you to death; and Yo-Yo, who wasn't even a Christian! Not to mention women from Jamaica, Honduras, South Africa—practically a mini-United Nations. We certainly didn't have much in common.

But something happened that weekend to make us realize we had to hang together. So "the Yada Yada Prayer Group" decided to keep praying for each other via e-mail. Our personal struggles and requests soon got too intense for cyberspace, so we decided to meet together every other Sunday night.

Talk about a rock tumbler!—knocking off each other's rough edges, learning to laugh and cry along the way. But when I faced the biggest crisis of my life, God used my newfound girlfriends to help teach me—Jodi Baxter, longtime Christian "good girl"—what it means to be just a sinner saved by grace.

THE YADA YADA PRAYER GROUP
ISBN 1-59145-074-8

AVAILABLE WHEREVER BOOKS ARE SOLD

BOOK 2

When they get shaken up, The Yada Yada Prayer Group Gets Down

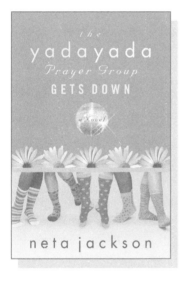

I had never felt so violated! The Yada Yada Prayer Group was "gettin' down" with God in prayer and praise one night when a heroin-crazed woman barged into my house, demanded our valuables and threatened us with a 10-inch knife—a knife that drew blood.

We wondered if we'd ever get back to normal after this terrifying experience. I assumed we would (although "normal" doesn't usually describe the 12 of us mismatched women anyway). After all, we'd been through a lot already as spiritual sisters. This was just one more hurdle to conquer, right?

But then a well-meaning gesture suddenly incited a backlash of anger in the group, forcing us to confront generations of racial division, pain and distrust—and stretching our friendships to the limit. Initially I thought, Surely I, Jodi "Good Girl" Baxter, am not responsible for other people's sins—am I? But a shocking confrontation in my third-grade classroom forced me to face my own accountability, and God used the Yada Yada Prayer Group (and my own husband, of all people) to show me what true forgiveness really is.

THE YADA YADA PRAYER GROUP GETS DOWN
ISBN 1-59145-151-5

AVAILABLE WHEREVER BOOKS ARE SOLD

BOOK 3

The Yada Yada Prayer Group Gets Real about Forgiveness

After everything the Yada Yadas had been through in the past eight months, I told God I could sure use a little "dull and boring" in the New Year! Was that too much to ask? But that was before Leslie "Stu" Stewart moved in upstairs. Ms. Perfect herself and me—Jodi Baxter—living in the same two-flat? A recipe for a collision. Then Delores Enriques' son Jose wanted to throw my Amanda a quinceañera—a coming-out party, Mexican style—and they're only fifteen!

Yo-Yo's still making us squirm with her gut-level honesty . . . and what's with this guy courting Avis? *Our* Avis! I guess I should have realized that with 11 Yada Yada sisters as diverse as a bag of Jelly Bellies, life would always be unpredictable.

At least Bandana Woman, who held up our Yada Yada Prayer Group at knifepoint last fall, was safely locked up in prison . . . or so I thought. We visited her, like the Bible says; even sent her something for Christmas. But then she ends up back in our face. I mean, how far is forgiveness supposed to go?

All I know is that the longer we Yada Yadas pray together, the more "real" things are getting, not only with each other but with God. "Dull and boring"? Not a chance!

THE YADA YADA PRAYER GROUP GETS REAL

ISBN 1-59145-152-3

AVAILABLE WHEREVER BOOKS ARE SOLD